'CAP's work amongst the poor and margina... ...UK ...s inspirational and really needed at this time. We beli... ...changes lives and through this charity, many despera... ...ountered the love of God in a practical and life-transf... ...e testimonies represent just a few of the people who have ... ...hope where before there was none. CAP truly is transforming con... ...ies one life at a time.'

– Andy Hawthorne, CEO & Founder of The Message Trust

'Debt tears families apart and drives individuals to desperation. It is one of the most pressing problems facing our society today. I am so thankful for the work of CAP and the thousands of people whose lives have been transformed through that work. I am inspired when I read about people who have been given a way through their financial trauma, regained their dignity and, most importantly, received hope. If ever there was a time that the church in the UK needed to take action on personal debt it is now – and CAP enables the church to effectively meet this most pressing of needs.'

– ROB PARSONS, Care for the Family

JOURNEYS OF HOPE

12 **LIVES** CHANGED BY **GOD**

CHRISTIANS AGAINST POVERTY BOOKS

Bradford

CONTENTS

	Acknowledgements	7
	Introduction by Matt & Josie Barlow	9
	How CAP Works	15
1.	New Life: Mark & Lyndsay	17
2.	Peace: Christine	31
3.	Bright Future: Lloyd	45
4.	Transformation: Ralph	53
5.	Wholeness: Susan	63
6.	Revelation: Phil & Zoe	75
7.	Justice Fulfilled: Andy	89
8.	Freedom: Julia	103
9.	Faith: Emily & Nigel	115
10.	A Love To Share: Pam	125
11.	New Family: Beverley	137
12.	Marriage Restored: Pete & Maxine	149
	Epilogue by John Kirkby	161
	Life Changer Forms	165
	How Can I Become A Christian?	173

ACKNOWLEDGEMENTS

By Jonathan Priestley & Tina Morris

We would like to thank everyone who has shared their wonderful stories. It's not easy to make yourself vulnerable by describing some of the darkest moments of your life and we appreciate your courage. We pray that you will be blessed by sharing your story with us. As writers of this book, it has been our privilege to meet wonderful people with truly spectacular stories.

Secondly, we would like to thank our Design Team, Nicola Robinson and Claire Cowles, for designing and then type-setting this book – a long and boring task by any stretch of the imagination. Thank you for giving your time to do this and doing it in such a great spirit!

Thanks also goes to our manager, Josie Barlow. Josie is an amazing leader and driver of our team. Her encouragement and wisdom has been invaluable – we really couldn't have written this without her.

To end, we would like to give all glory to God. Hearing each person's individual journey has been such an inspiration. God is truly an awesome God. In so many situations he has reached into the darkness, bringing hope, peace, healing and salvation to people in desperate situations. All praise to God, the restorer and bringer of hope.

We pray you enjoy this book.

God bless.

Jonathan and Tina

Jonathan Priestley

Jonathan Priestley is our PR Officer. Since arriving at CAP in January 2008, he has transformed the PR of the charity by empowering local centres to raise their profile in their communities and seeing CAP's name become more prominent in the Christian and national press. During his time at CAP, Jonathan has been encouraged and inspired by the lives transformed as a result of God's and CAP's intervention.

Tina Morris

Tina Morris started working at Christians Against Poverty in December 2004. Since then, God has taken her from strength to strength, challenging and inspiring her about what he can do with broken lives. Tina works as the Executive Assistant to Matt Barlow and John Kirkby, in addition to working alongside Josie Barlow to fundraise from charitable trusts.

Josie & Matt with their two children, Jed & Eve.

INTRODUCTION

By Matt & Josie Barlow

I walked up the path to Julia's new house, it was a sunny day and having spoken to her on the phone I was really looking forward to meeting her. This is one of the best parts of my job. Julia gave me a massive hug and was radiant as she showed me round her lovely house.

Talking to her, I felt my spirit rise as I heard how Owen (CAP's Hemel Hempstead Centre Manager) had walked into her life, bringing light, peace and calm when she was at her most desperate. She described how she felt God had come into the room with Owen and how she knew that everything would now be alright with God as her guiding light. Julia told me she has found friends and a new family at church, and that she is now a Support Worker for CAP, helping other people out of the same awful situation that she has been in herself.

God works through people. He has decided to show himself to the world not through big impressive displays but through people's changed lives. People who he loves, people who he wants as part of his family, people who he died for. Ordinary people, like a divorced lady who was deeply depressed and not coping with mounting debts that in the end made her and her two children homeless. People like Julia.

This book tells twelve stories of people who have met God through the work of Christians Against Poverty and as a result have had their lives completely turned around. For some, their stories will tell how God has lifted them out of a pit of debt and misery and placed their feet on a rock of hope and love. For others, it will be how they have found a way to bring God's justice and compassion to those he loves the most by working for CAP. The latter of these is what happened to Matt and I.

As a child, watching Live Aid and the famines in Ethiopia gave me a strong desire to get out there one day and help people out of poverty. I went to Lancaster University, where I met this very tall boy in a salmon coloured shirt and deep red Doc Martins. He looked like he owned the place even though we'd only been there a few months. At the time, Matt wasn't a Christian, but after a few months, he asked God to show him if he was real. God showed up big time in Matt's room and he became a 'fully going for it' follower of Jesus. He was on fire for God. After university, we both wanted to help people who were living in poverty, so we spent the next two years in the Dominican Republic living in a poor village near the Haitian border. The charity we were working for provided an amazing primary school, ambulance service and rural clinic. We had two of the best years of our lives, living with amazing people who had such a joy for life despite having so little.

On our return, we were wondering how to carry on the call on our lives to help people out of poverty and see them come into a relationship with God, when John Kirkby showed up in our church in Cheltenham at the end of 1997. After hearing about CAP, our pastor thought Matt would be good as a CAP Centre Manager. So with an open mind, Matt went up to Bradford to meet John.

When John heard about us, our heart and what we had been doing, he felt we were an answer to prayer. They had been asking God for two people to join CAP. One was to help oversee the new centre network, as CAP Aldershot had just opened and four more centres were planned for January. John thought Matt would be great in this role. CAP was also looking for someone to concentrate on fundraising. As I had been doing fundraising in my job in Cheltenham, John offered us both jobs! After visiting John and his wife Lizzie, we knew this was an amazing opportunity. So within six weeks we were living in Bradford and had joined the five staff working for CAP in two bedrooms in John's old house.

It has been such a privilege to have been here from the beginning and to have been part of the amazing adventure of Christians Against Poverty. We have had a few cuts and bruises along the way and we have regularly been on our knees without the money to pay staff salaries, but we totally trust our God. He is our guide and has always provided for us in the end!

Our vision, our summit, will be when we have a CAP Centre in every town and city so that anyone suffering in debt and the misery it causes can find a solution. It's amazing what can happen when you align yourself with God's mission and heart for the poor and the lost. He wants CAP to grow and to reach more and more people. It's no wonder that we now have so many centres open in partnership with local churches, helping hundreds of people out of debt every month – with at least one person becoming a part of God's family every day.

What drives us on is knowing how horrendous life is for so many people in our communities, and that we really do have a solution that works. Our sophisticated debt counselling service is the solution for money and debt issues, and provides an opportunity to know the God who loves them. By partnering with the local church, people can discover a new family and find friends. We know there is hope. Debt, misery and suicide don't have to be the end of the journey. God can transform any situation, no matter how desperate, and we have seen him do it time and time again.

Matt & Josie Barlow

Matt and Josie came to CAP in 1999. They were married in 1997 and have two children, Eve and Jed. Matt is the UK Chief Executive for CAP, being appointed in 2006 after spending seven years building the systems and infrastructure to support CAP's growth. Such is Matt's leadership abilities that he was awarded 'Best Leader' at the Sunday Times' 'Best Small Companies to Work For' 2008.

Josie is Head of Communications at CAP. She is a highly experienced fundraiser who brings a wealth of creativity, enthusiasm and drive to the team. They are a dynamic couple who are one hundred per cent committed to the poor and lost of this nation. Passionate about justice for the oppressed, Matt and Josie are excited to be part of a charity that is truly speaking up for those who cannot speak for themselves.

HOW CAP WORKS

A t Christians Against Poverty we are committed to offering the very best service to those with the very least. We give the most comprehensive service in the UK and it really works! We don't just help people for a few weeks, we support them until they are debt free, even if it takes years. This is truly relieving poverty over the long haul.

So, how does CAP get people out of debt?

Step 1 – Home Visits:

After calling CAP's freephone number and booking an appointment, each client is visited in their own home several times by a Debt Advisor and Support Worker from their local CAP Centre.

Step 2 – An Effective Budget:

CAP's specialised departments at Head Office then work out a realistic budget by prioritising essential bills and negotiating affordable payments with each creditor. This is to stop interest and charges.

Step 3 – The CAP Account:

A CAP Account, which acts like a simple bank account, is set up. The client makes one weekly or monthly payment into their account that covers all their bills and debts, which we then distribute on their behalf. Provision is also made in this account for savings, a key to long-term poverty relief.

Step 4 – Insolvency (Bankruptcy):

If a client is in severe debt then we can walk them through insolvency options. We help our clients at every step of the journey from filling out forms to attending court with them.

Step 5 – Long-term Support:

Clients use their CAP Account to pay their bills and debts, and are supported by our CAP team until they are debt free. We will even continue to support clients after they are debt free, to help them remain on top of their finances.

Lyndsay, Mark and their two children with John Kirkby

1. NEW LIFE

Mark & Lyndsay's Story

Lyndsay's Story

I was shaking slightly as I held the pill bottle in my hand, wondering what to do. With two young children and only a couple of years into marriage, it should have been the happiest time of my life, but I was desperate. I felt alone, isolated, scared, depressed. Nothing I tried could shake off the feelings of insecurity I had. Who understood me? I couldn't talk to my husband, Mark; I found it impossible to open up and he probably wouldn't have understood me anyway. What was the answer to all this hurt, fear and pain?

I looked down at the pill bottle again, still clutching it tightly in my hand. Perhaps this was the only answer. It would be an end to all my problems once and for all. I wouldn't have to worry about money, about my lack of self-worth, about the difficulties with Mark. It would all be gone in an instant. I couldn't face being without the children, but what good was I to them when I was this depressed? There was no hope for us. I just couldn't face another day of fear and worry.

I unscrewed the cap of the bottle and tipped a couple of pills into my hand. I looked at them closely. Just a few small pills would take all this desperation away. A few small pills was all it would take. I tipped a few more onto the palm of my hand and counted them out; eight, nine, ten. Trembling in fear I took the first pill and placed it on my tongue. Then, taking a sip of water, I swallowed it down. That pill meant no more worries. The next pill went down more easily. No more financial difficulty. The third barely touched the sides as I swallowed. No more arguments with Mark. The fourth I hardly noticed. No more anxiety and insecurity. The fifth, the sixth, the seventh, then it all went black…

When I woke up in hospital I wasn't sure where I was. People were standing around, but I was still in a daze. I could barely see. Mark was there too, but I hardly recognised him. Then the shame suddenly hit me as I remembered what I'd done. How could I tell him that I'd rather die than carry on with our marriage? And the kids; what would they think? How could I say the words 'Mummy didn't want to live anymore'? The shame was massive, almost unbearable. I cringed inside and out. The doctors told me that if it had been any longer before I'd got to hospital, there would have been nothing they could have done. I had come so close to dying, but something had meant I was spared.

Then all the thoughts came rushing back, like someone had opened the floodgate of my memory; all the money worries, all the insecurity, all the desperation, all the depression. All the things I'd tried so hard to escape and all those mountains I felt I could never get over. It just hit me like a wave. I knew I was still alive for a reason, but I had no idea what that reason was. All I knew was that these problems needed to be sorted out. The thing was, they had stemmed all the way from my teenage years.

When I was pregnant with our eldest daughter, the doctors said there was a problem with her heart; that it was beating too fast. It made the pregnancy feel like I was walking a tightrope and I constantly had these 'what ifs' running through the back of my mind. What if she never made it? What if she was born with severe heart problems? What if I wasn't able to cope as a new mother? It was crushing; the tension was almost unbearable.

Thankfully, she was born healthy, but I suffered terrible post-natal depression. I think part of it was due to the stress of the pregnancy. By the time our second daughter was born two years later, the depression was still there and following her birth, it got even worse. When Mark and I married I had hoped that some of the problems would go away, but it just seemed to make them worse. We couldn't communicate and I felt so isolated. I switched off and shut down. I couldn't open up to him about the way I was feeling and I just wanted all the problems to go away.

Added to this were the money worries. The debt problems began when we rented a nice two-bedroom flat as a couple. We had been living with my mum in a large house, but there were so many of us it was impossible to get personal space. Mark and I wanted a nice family home with the kids. We were naïve and thought you just found the flat you wanted and said, 'We'll rent it.' News that we needed to put a deposit down on the flat came as a shock.

It wasn't a massive deposit, but £800 was beyond our reach at that time as we didn't have any savings. We'd never managed to get credit out but the bank was very keen to give us an overdraft to cover it. We jumped at the chance; we could be independent of my mum and also build a lovely family home for us and our two children. Little did we know that it would be the starting point for our financial crisis.

I had done plenty of catalogue shopping before and always managed to pay things off on time, but with the interest and payments on the overdraft, it really started to eat into our finances. Soon we weren't coping with the repayments and things started to spiral out of control. We weren't servicing our existing debt, let alone paying the rent and the overdraft. It was a desperate time and one of the main contributors to my attempted suicide. Although we had never argued about money, it was a real stress for me and a constant worry.

I don't think it's ever just one thing that drives someone to suicide, but a combination. For me, I couldn't take the endless assault of my insecurities, money worries and fear. It was too much for one person to take and I wanted out. Mark was distraught and I felt awful that I'd let him down, but with all my insecurities I just wasn't able to tell him how I was feeling and being able to trust was a total no-go. It was impossible for me to trust anybody and that included Mark. I would question everything he said and wonder whether he was lying to me, which created a real atmosphere of tension in the house. He really struggled too because he was desperate to convince me that he was trustworthy and that he loved me, but I just couldn't take it in. There was this barrier that he couldn't ever get behind and it must have caused him so much pain.

A couple of months before I tried to end it all, I had a brief chat with my aunt, who was a CAP client. She talked to me about the work of the charity and how it could help people like me. I thought it was interesting at the time, but I really wasn't desperate enough to take her up on the offer. Then my world totally fell apart and I took an overdose. I think everything just caught up with me. It's amazing how a crisis can make you think more clearly than you've ever thought before.

Once I had recovered enough to leave hospital, it was only a matter of weeks before I contacted Gemma, the Centre Manager at the CAP Centre in Walton to arrange a visit. I was so nervous before our first meeting in January 2008. I can remember sitting on the sofa with Mark, surrounded by our financial files.

We had managed to stay quite well organised in spite of the financial worries and difficulties. I had a file with all my expenses in, Mark had his own file and then we had a joint file too. Still, I was worried that Gemma would come in and be shocked about how badly we had managed our finances.

With the shame of the suicide, I was also worried about the shame of failing financially. What would Gemma say? I secretly hoped that she wouldn't be judgemental, but I feared the worse. As a car pulled up outside our house, my heart raced. I nervously went over to the window and peered out. I could see a woman, about the same age as me, sitting in the driver's seat and looking through various files and then closing her eyes. She looked like she was talking to someone. I thought it was a little strange, but I went back to sit on the sofa and wait to see whether she knocked at the door. I glanced at Mark. I could tell by the look on his face that he was equally nervous.

It seemed like ages but she finally approached our house and knocked at the door. I wondered what she'd been doing in the car and as I went to answer the door I felt sick with nerves. As I opened it, a young woman just stood there beaming at me. She smiled, held out her hand to shake mine and said 'Hi, I'm Gemma from CAP.' We welcomed her in without really knowing what to expect, but looking back, that meeting was one of the most amazing experiences I'd ever had. It was such a relief to chat to her about our finances and the difficulty we had got into. We handed everything over to her, including the three files and nervously waited to see what she made of them. To our surprise, she said how well organised we were and that previously she'd left homes with bin bags full of bank statements, bills and court orders!

That made me feel more reassured about things, but the greatest relief of all was to hear that Gemma would now be looking after our finances and helping us whilst we paid off the debt in manageable monthly payments. I now had hope that the finances could be sorted out. I could finally breathe again and I could tell that Mark was relieved too. The best news of all was when the financial plan came back from CAP's head office and it showed that we could spend £100 on food a week, because we had two children. That meant we wouldn't have to live on the cheapest, smallest amount of food just to get by;

we could enjoy eating healthily again without worrying about not paying back the debt. Over time the threatening letters stopped coming through the post too. That made such a difference to the quality of our lives.

With our finances now under control, it gave me space to consider the other problems that had been plaguing me. The insecurities were still there and I wondered whether I would ever shake them off. I still found it almost impossible to trust Mark and I knew that this needed to be sorted out, otherwise it would be the end of our marriage. The truth is, if the husband won't trust the wife or the wife refuses to trust the husband, a marriage is doomed and ours was looking worse than ever.

Out of the blue, a few months into working with CAP, Gemma invited us to a special night she was putting on for her clients and those from the other Liverpool CAP Centre. I was a little suspicious at first, but decided to go along and so did Mark. It seemed like a really kind gesture, although I was unsure about what was going to happen that evening. I felt very nervous but once I'd arrived found it reassuring to meet other clients who were being helped by CAP.

There was food to eat and the CAP Support Workers were so lovely. It really blew me away how nice everyone was. I was unprepared for what would happen next, though. I just thought it was going to be a relaxed evening and the chance to meet some more CAP clients. Part of the evening was spent watching a short film called 'Rain' from Rob Bell at NOOMA[1]. I can remember in the film the fact that he was

[1]NOOMA DVDs are short films that explain life issues from a Christian perspective, using language and images that are relevant to modern society. At CAP we often use these DVDs to communicate Christianity to our clients. www.nooma.com.

walking through the forest in the rain with his baby son on his back in a baby carrier. The rain was pelting down and his son was becoming more and more anxious and started to scream and cry.

So Rob Bell said to his child, 'Everything's going to be OK, buddy. Daddy's here and he loves you.' I was holding Mark's hand at the time. Then, all of a sudden, I felt this massive squeeze around my middle, but it wasn't like someone was giving me a hug from the outside, but a hug from the inside. It wasn't painful but the pressure was intense. I squeezed Mark's hand as I thought I was going to pass out. It was a strange experience but after a few seconds it went and I was left a bit stunned by the whole thing.

I plucked up the courage to speak to Gemma about it, as it was such a bizarre experience. She asked me really directly, 'You know who it was, don't you? It was God giving you a hug'. 'Yes, I guess so,' I replied and inside I knew it was true. Then, quick as a flash she asked, 'Well, what's stopping you from becoming a Christian then?' and I said the words 'well nothing, really.' As they tumbled out of my mouth, I was surprised by how easily I said them and how much I believed it to be true.

In what seemed like a matter of seconds, about five people had gathered round to pray with me. We sat down and I asked God into my life, said sorry for the wrong things I'd done and asked his forgiveness. I felt absolutely amazing after that, like I was floating on air for the rest of the evening. It was like I was lifted up and walking taller than everyone else. People kept saying to me, 'You're glowing, you're glowing.' I felt incredible and went to bed that night so happy and peaceful.

The following morning when I woke up, I still felt overwhelming joy and peace. It was like someone had reached into my brain and removed all the insecurities I felt and all the worry. When you have these insecurities, it doesn't matter how happy you are in the moment, they're always there, at the back of you mind. The amazing thing was, they'd gone. Totally gone! I still struggle with them from time to time but now I know that I have the support and love of God to help me deal with them. He has turned my life around and I can't put into words how much of a help the love and support of CAP has been too.

Mark's Story

When Lyndsay became a Christian, I couldn't get over the change in her. She was on a high for a few months afterwards and it totally changed our relationship. Before, it had been impossible for me to convince her that I loved her and that she could trust me but now we're able to communicate and we're building a stronger relationship as each week goes by. It obviously hasn't always been that easy, though.

Seeing her in hospital after the overdose was one of the most horrific experiences of my life. I can remember the pain and trauma like it was yesterday. It was like she was behind a bullet-proof screen. I could see her and communicate with her but I couldn't reach her. It was desperate. Nothing I said or did would break the barrier down. She always questioned what I said, thought I was lying and would find it impossible to trust me.

I was so close to giving up hope and with the money problems it got even worse. We were slipping further and further into debt and when Lyndsay took an overdose I knew that things had reached crisis point. With two young children and a beautiful wife, I tried so hard to hold it all together but I wasn't able to. When we approached CAP for help, it really was our last chance, as previous companies who had promised the same service hadn't delivered. CAP really was all we had left to try.

Meeting Gemma for the first time was such a nerve-wracking experience. I can picture that day now, with me and Lyndsay sitting nervously on the sofa waiting for the knock at the door, surrounded by our files and a mountain of questions.

When Gemma did finally come to the door and introduce herself, we were shocked by how friendly, calm and un judgemental she was. We had expected someone to come into our house and really tell us off for the way that we had been handling our finances, but from Gemma we got reassurance, love and a good deal of patience too. When we said goodbye to her after that meeting I was so relieved. I finally felt like there was someone who understood our financial situation and who could help us. I was desperate and although I didn't admit it to Lyndsay at the time I was sure there was no way out for us. Gemma's visit gave me hope again.

Gemma was amazing and when she came back with the financial statement, I was bowled over that we could pay off our debt in a good period of time, still eat properly and save money too. It was fantastic to worry less about the money side of things and when the threatening letters slowed down and stopped I knew the financial plan was working. I was relieved about our finances, but I knew things between Lyndsay and me were still tough and all the insecurities she had were still there.

When Gemma invited us to the client evening, I have to confess I was pretty dubious. I know Lyndsay was really nervous, but I was more suspicious about the whole thing and wasn't sure whether we would enjoy ourselves or not. When we arrived it was actually reassuring to see the other clients and nice to have some food together and have our photo taken. I felt a bit more relaxed and sat down with Lyndsay to watch the 'Rain' DVD by NOOMA. We were holding hands at the time, a sign that things had started to improve between us.

Half way through the DVD Lyndsay suddenly started to squeeze my hand really tight. I wasn't sure why at the time and thought it was a bit strange but then she shared about how she felt squeezed in her middle when Rob Bell was talking about comforting his baby son. She spoke to Gemma a few minutes after and all of a sudden people gathered round and Lyndsay became a Christian. I'd like to say I was shocked by it all, but secretly I wasn't. It felt right at the time and whilst I'd never formally made a commitment to be a Christian, I did pray from time to time.

Seeing the change in Lyndsay afterwards was pretty amazing, though. She looked so different; her eyes changed and her face was literally glowing; people kept coming up to her and saying that as the evening drew to a close. The following morning when she woke up she shared about how the insecurities that had plagued her for so long were gone. I was amazed and relieved. It was like someone had lifted a weight from my shoulders. I knew at that point that there was hope for our relationship, that we were able to move forward as a couple. It was mind-blowing to see the change in her and she was on a high for several months after. After years of trying to convince her that I loved her, she was able to accept it. She had changed from the inside out. I was still not sure about being a Christian, though.

We'd never been on a holiday as just the four of us, so when Gemma invited us to go on a Discovery Break to Hayes, Swanwick, we jumped at the chance. It was a free holiday and a much-needed break from all the stress and trauma of the past six months. Lyndsay and I were really looking forward to it, but as the day got closer, we became a little more nervous. We were going to be staying with other CAP clients and some of the staff too and I wasn't sure what to make of the idea. Whilst I'd seen an amazing change in Lyndsay, I was pretty convinced I didn't want to commit to being a Christian and was concerned about them trying to make me.

We didn't know anyone when we arrived, but Lyndsay spotted Matt Barlow out of the corner of her eye. She said to me in a joking way 'he's weird, that one,' but apart from the dodgy Scouse accent he tried to do, we got to know him and his wife, Josie, really well over the course of the four days. They were so kind to us and we've since struck up a great friendship with them. We also made friends with a Scottish family too and that helped us to settle in to the break a bit more easily as we'd eat with them at mealtimes.

Ever since I was a child, I'd always had a faith that God existed and I used to pray to him from time to time, but I never had the faith to believe in Christianity. Seeing the change in Lyndsay convinced me that it was the right faith, but I just wanted to become a Christian at the right time. On the second night we watched the video 'Rain' by Rob Bell and I think Lyndsay was secretly hoping I'd get a 'God Hug' whilst watching it too. Nothing happened and I think she was a little disappointed, but we broke into small groups towards the end of the night to discuss what we'd seen. Josie was leading the discussion in our group, but no-one else was talking and I couldn't stand sitting there in silence, so I started to speak. 'I'm not a Christian yet,' I started. 'I do believe, but it's just not the right time to make a commitment.'

Josie came back quick as a flash and said, 'It sounds like you're the kind of person that needs to think things through thoroughly before making a decision, like you need to rationalise everything.' That challenged me, but I still wasn't prepared to make a commitment to follow Jesus. I didn't want to disappoint Lyndsay, but I knew it had to be the right time and I wasn't going to bow to pressure. Later on that night, we were sitting in a group with some other people having a drink and Matt came over to join us. When we started talking about Christianity and whether we had faith in Jesus, I said, 'I'm not a Christian yet, but it is a four-day break!' Matt asked me why I hadn't yet become a Christian and I suddenly felt convicted that I needed to pray the prayer of salvation.

Becoming a Christian was the most life-transforming decision I have ever made. Not only has it brought me closer to Lyndsay, but I now have this incredible relationship with God where I know I can rely on him for my strength. Our two beautiful daughters also became Christians on that Discovery Break too and I'm amazed at how God has saved us as a family.

My new relationship with God is great and I'm learning how to pray as well. Sometimes when I pray out loud, the words don't seem to make sense, but in my head they do! It's amazing how God can restore where it feels like so much has been taken away from you. When Lyndsay took her overdose, I never believed that we would be able to pull through. There was just so much hurt, pain and difficulty to overcome. God gave us the strength and through CAP he made himself known to us and showed us how much he loves us. It's amazing to think that as a family we now have hope for the future and we're part of a new family with other Christians.

We recently stayed at Matt and Josie's house whilst they were away on holiday. It was such a fantastic break and nice to get away from Liverpool for a few days. Lyndsay said to Josie and Matt that she wanted to swap lives with them. Matt replied that we couldn't swap lives, but that we could come and be a part of theirs and that's the way I'd sum up being a Christian, really; being part of the most incredible family you could ever imagine, with God as the parent you always wanted.

Christine & Jimmy.

2. PEACE

Christine's Story

It's still early in the morning and as I look out of the bedroom window, the sun has just come up. I can hear the birds singing, but for me it's not a happy sound; just a reminder that I've got to face another day. Even though I'm wide awake, I can't stomach getting up, getting dressed and leaving the house. Not yet anyway. I feel so ill and besides, who would I go and see? I put my slippers on, tie my old, tatty dressing gown around me and glance at the clock on my bedside table.

It's 6:30 and the rest of the world still seems to be sound asleep. There's no use trying to lie-in, even though I have nothing to do. I can't remember the last time I slept well, let alone the last time I didn't wake up in the middle of the night in a panic. My husband, Jimmy, is still asleep, but I'm in no mood to wake him up. I know he's worried about our situation, but I just wish he was able to do something about it. I feel powerless too, though. I've lost hope of being able to get out of this and it makes me so angry I just want to scream.

I shuffle my way downstairs to the living room and put the TV on and wonder whether I can stick another day of this misery. I collapse on the sofa, yawning as I go. I feel slightly sick. As the TV springs to life, I think about my life and what I've become. I'm a middle-aged woman slumped in front of the TV, trapped in my own home hiding this dark secret. I hate myself and what I've become. I haven't spoken to Jimmy, properly in days. When I bring up money, it seems to end in an argument and its stopping us from talking. I feel so full of anger it stops all the other emotions from coming out. I wish I was able to tell him that I loved him, but I've never been able to say those three little words out loud; not in over thirty-five years of marriage.

Then, all of a sudden, another pang of sickness hits me and I reach for my handbag which is by the side of the sofa. Almost in autopilot, I place my hand inside and feel for the small black case whilst still keeping my eyes fixed on the TV. Finding it, I pull it out and place it on my lap, pausing slightly to change the channel on the TV. There is never anything on at this time and this morning is no different. I unzip the case and look at the needle inside. I sigh. 'How many injections today?' I wonder to myself.

I put the needle beside me on the sofa and stand up slowly, still feeling awful and not sure whether I'm going to make it to the kitchen or not. Shuffling my way towards the kitchen door like a zombie, I wonder whether anyone else has to live like this. I feel so ashamed and I have to stop myself from welling up. If my family saw me like this, they'd be shocked. Only our younger son knows about the situation as he lives with us, but it's a total secret to everyone else.

My heart sinks as I prepare to open the kitchen cupboards. What am I going to find in there? Money is so tight that we can't afford to eat properly and all the cheap, sugary and fatty foods mean I can't control my diabetes. I just feel ill the whole time and can't regulate my blood-sugar levels. The tiredness is almost too much to take but I just can't sleep. It's a waking nightmare.

Looking through the cupboards, I face the daily challenge of how I'm going to feed us without spending more money. Most dinners it's just the same; chips, chips or chips. If we are lucky, we might have a fried egg too. I can count on one hand the number of times over the past two weeks that we've eaten meat. It's so depressing. I long for an invite over to our son's for a Sunday roast. All that meat and vegetables. I can imagine the smell now. I have to stop thinking about that though. It's time for breakfast and I need to feed myself before I go into a diabetic coma...

My name is Christine and I live in Dunfermline. I moved up from Huddersfield seven and a half years ago with my husband and family to mend my relationship with my sister. I had a traumatic upbringing and as a result, Jimmy and I left Scotland, where we had both been born and raised and moved to Yorkshire as his aunt lived there. We escaped in more ways than one, you could say. We were financially stable when we lived in Yorkshire and had no debt when we arrived in Scotland. That would all change though. I shudder to think how difficult life was when we'd moved back.

Jimmy couldn't find work when we returned to Scotland. He'd previously been a potato grader. It was awful work and didn't pay great. It gave him terrible pain in his shoulders which he'd often complain of when he got back at the end of the day. I was desperate to think of a solution, but we needed the money. Day after day he'd come back, totally exhausted. Day after day, I'd desperately rack my brains, trying to think of a way out. One day it all got too much. Jimmy stopped work as it was just too painful for him. I don't blame him at all; it must have been awful and I felt terrible that he'd been in so much agony because of his job.

It was this pain that stopped him from working when we came back to Scotland and it was impossible to support the household on the small amount of benefits we got. I'd had diabetes for some time and I was finding it harder and harder to regulate my blood-sugar levels. As the money dried up, so did the variety in our diet. The weekly shop was a never-ending battle of wills between what I needed to stay healthy and what we could afford. All the cheap food was full of fat and sugar and so bad for my health, but I had no choice if we wanted to keep some kind of financial control.

My health really suffered as I put on weight and my blood-sugar rocketed. I felt constantly ill and wondered when it was all going to end. When I woke up in the mornings, I'd feel instantly unwell and wonder how I'd have the strength to get through the day. It wasn't just the monotony of our lives, but the daily struggle that really ground me down. The anger was still there, simmering under the surface, and it wouldn't take much for me to lose my temper with people.

If someone in the street gave me so much as a dodgy look I'd be straight up to them in an instant. If I thought Jimmy had been disrespected that made me even angrier. My language was terrible as well. Inside I was desperate. I found it harder and harder to shoulder the burden of our finances. I knew that Jimmy felt totally powerless to get us out of the situation, but I struggled because I felt I was left to deal with it myself. We were slipping deeper and deeper into difficulty and I would get really worried about it. I'd try to protect Jimmy from it because I knew he got unsettled if he saw me anxious, but sometimes I just couldn't hide my feelings.

Then, when there were no options left open to us, we took out a doorstep loan. Looking back, I wished I'd never done it, but I was so desperate and I knew Jimmy was unlikely ever to find work again. A doorstep lender knocked on our door one day and I think I just crumbled under the pressure of everything. It was against my better judgement, but when you're that hard pressed I think you'd do anything to escape your situation. The loan gave us a little bit of financial freedom, but that soon evaporated when we realised how much the interest and repayments would cost. It was a thin veneer of happiness and I knew it wouldn't last, so it was no surprise that we ended up in a worse financial state than before. I was seething with anger I could barely control. I blamed Jimmy for the situation we were in. I felt trapped and forced into getting the loan from the doorstep lender and now I felt like it was resting on my shoulders.

It didn't take long for the loan company to start harrassing us. First of all, it was just the odd knock at the door, but then it got worse. The phone barely stopped ringing, but the company used different numbers to call so I never knew if it was them or not. When I answered the phone, I'd find out it was them and then I'd feel stupid for picking up. It was a nightmare and throughout it all I still wanted desperately for Jimmy to sort it out, but I knew neither of us were able to. When I did start talking about finance, it was like he glazed over. I ended up feeling resentful, but I think it was just desperation because secretly I was crying out for him to express his fear and pain like I was. It was like the lights had gone out and there was no-one to save us.

In the midst of all the pain and the health problems I was having, we considered how we would be able to support ourselves financially as the benefits barely stretched to our budget and the doorstep loan repayments were absolutely crippling. Because we were a household on minimal income and no salary, the only thing the bank could offer us was a flexi-loan. It sounded like a fantastic idea at the time and the fact that it came from a bank made me believe that they would deal with us more humanely than the doorstep lenders. How wrong I was. Because we had an absolutely awful credit rating, it turned out that this flexi-loan was really just like a credit card in disguise.

I felt like such a fool, like I'd been tricked into it and then our financial situation just got worse and worse. Now we had the doorstep lender on our backs and constantly calling at the door and also the bank issuing us with horrific interest. It was a nightmare. I wanted to scream and run away. I felt like a caged animal and I couldn't bear it. I just wanted to kick and punch and scratch my way out of this life and end it all. I wanted Jimmy to wave a magic wand and make all the money problems, all the pain and all the anger go away. The truth is, although I'd never said it, I did love him and I just couldn't express it because I was so full of anger.

Throughout all of this, our extended family and friends never knew the situation we'd got into. I think they were probably aware that there were some financial worries, but if they'd known there was barely any food in the house, save some dirt-cheap chips, they'd have been shocked. It was so humiliating. I wanted to curl up and die. We were dragging ourselves from one day to the next, robbing Peter to pay Paul.

One Thursday morning I was sitting on the sofa, wondering what on earth we were going to do. I had the local paper next to me and I opened it up to have a read. On one of the pages, there was an advert for a charity called 'Christians Against Poverty'. It said they did debt counselling and that they had a centre in Dunfermline that would help people in financial difficulty. I thought to myself 'Well, I've never seen a poor Christian, perhaps they could help us.' I mentioned it to Jimmy and to my surprise, he was quite keen on the idea and suggested that I give them a call. When I called up Julie, the Centre Manager, I really didn't know what to expect. I hadn't been inside a church since my childhood and the thought of welcoming a Christian into our house was a bit strange, but she seemed so nice on the phone and we arranged a time for her to come round.

Having kept our financial crisis a secret from the rest of the family, it was unsettling to welcome a stranger into our home to talk about our deepest and darkest fear. Still, I think we'd reached desperation point at this stage and I looked on Julie as our last hope. If it didn't work out, I had no idea what else to do. When she knocked at the door, I suddenly felt overwhelmed with shame and paused before going to answer, but I took the plunge and opened it.

When you're in debt, the most crippling feelings are shame and fear. It was the shame of our financial situation that made me want to hide away and cry. I was really frightened about how Julie would react because my family didn't know and Jimmy and I had never let anyone else in on our secret. I could imagine her saying, 'You fools, what were you thinking of?' and, 'There's no way on earth we can sort out this mess.' The amazing thing was that she never judged us. I remember that first meeting so well. I just wanted to cry the whole time, but it wasn't through sadness, it was because of the relief. Julie never criticised us or made us feel stupid for the mess we'd gotten into and she was never unkind. All she showed us was love and understanding. It was like she'd known us forever.

We didn't have a massive amount of debt, but because we were on benefits, it was so hard to make the books balance and we couldn't do it. Towards the end of the first visit, Julie offered to pray with us. I was really dubious at first. My Gran was a Salvationist and I used to go to chapel with her when I stayed at her house over the weekend. My dad was pretty anti-church though, so he wouldn't be happy about that. He always went to the pub instead of church and persuaded me that it wasn't a good idea to go along. Over the years I never had contact with Christians, let alone set foot in a church, so it was all new to me. I used to cry out to God in a crisis, but I didn't know who he was or what he was like. It was a desperation thing that made me want to cry out but I'd never say that I was a Christian. Still, Julie was so nice and kind to us that I thought it would be silly to stop her from praying. It was one of those moments that would change my life forever.

We closed our eyes and I can remember thinking 'what on earth am I doing?' I guess it was the hopelessness of the situation that made me want to reach out to God. Julie started to pray and the most amazing thing happened. As she was saying the words, I felt this incredible and enormous heat all over my body. The thing about it was that the heat didn't burn, but it felt almost comforting. I thought it was really strange and I didn't know what the heck was going on! When Julie finished praying, I just sat in the seat, stunned by what had just happened but too embarrassed to bring it up. A few minutes later, Julie left, and took all our statements with her. She promised to put together a plan that would help us pay back our debt in manageable chunks. That would mean I would be able to eat properly again and start to control my diabetes too.

She came back the following Monday and brought our new budget with her. It was fantastic. I can remember looking at it and being so overjoyed that we could afford to eat a good diet and that our new CAP Account meant we only had to make one payment a month and CAP would sort out the rest. I was happy with the budget and was still thinking about the strange heat I felt when we first prayed. Julie had left a little booklet called 'Why Jesus?' after our first meeting and I'd read through it because I wanted to find out more about God and why I'd felt this heat.

I felt nervous about bringing it up, but I plucked up the courage and asked her about why I'd felt it when she was praying. I half expected her to turn around and tell me that I had gone crazy, but she was really reassuring. 'That was God's Spirit, Christine,' she said, almost without thinking about it. Then, out of the blue, she asked another question to

Jimmy and me that I never thought someone would ask us. 'Would you like to become Christians?' Jimmy and I had been so overwhelmed with Julie's kindness. We couldn't understand how someone could be so loving and caring to strangers and especially people who were in so much need. As a couple, we were so amazed that it made us wonder about God and Jesus. The 'Why Jesus?' booklet had really challenged us too. Since the strange heat incident, God had really been preparing my heart and also Jimmy's.

We both said 'Yes' to Julie and what followed was the most incredible experience. Julie led us in a short prayer, where we said sorry for the things we'd done wrong and asked Jesus into our lives. When we had got to the end of the prayer, I felt this incredible peace. It was a deeper peace than I'd ever felt before. When you're in debt, it's impossible to find peace in your situation. The constant phone calls, harassment, worry and fear means you feel anything but peace, but this was incredible. I felt so emotional, like I'd been waiting for this my whole life and Jimmy felt the same too. To know God loved me was the most amazing thing. Before we became Christians, Julie would say 'Don't let this rob you of your peace,' but I would always think to myself, 'What peace? I don't feel any peace.' When we became Christians, I knew true peace for the first time and I changed from the inside out.

When Julie left, she promised to come back on Wednesday to see how we were getting on. Both Jimmy and I were really excited about the commitment we'd made and wondered how our lives were going to unfold. I couldn't wait to see Julie again but nothing prepared me for what happened that Wednesday. When the doorbell rang, I went to answer it without that terrible fear I used to feel. I always used to worry about it being a debt collector or someone with bad news, but this time I went to the door with confidence. I expected to see

Julie with her file and nothing else, but I had the shock of my life when I turned the handle and opened the door. She was standing on the doorstep with bags full to bursting with food. 'I've done a shop for you,' she said, 'Because you didn't have much food in the house.' At that point, I cried. All the emotion just came pouring out of me, in torrents of tears. They weren't tears of sadness though, but tears of relief and joy. Before I was a Christian I never would have been able to express my emotion like that, but Jesus had melted my heart and replaced my anger with peace.

No one had ever been so kind to us before and I couldn't believe Julie had come back with so much food. Our cupboards were nearly bare and secretly I was frightened that we were going to run out of food before our CAP budget kicked in, so Julie's kindness came just at the right time. She was like an angel to us. Julie took us with her the first time we went to the church a few weeks later. I really didn't know what to expect but I knew that God was doing something amazing in our lives and I wanted to respond to him. Jimmy and I really enjoyed our first visit and left wanting more. We were really impacted by how kind and caring all the people there were. We thought maybe it was just Julie who could be that kind, but going to church showed us that it wasn't just her!

Jimmy and I plucked up the courage to go by ourselves on the following Sunday morning as Julie wasn't around to take us. That in itself was a major step for us and proof that Jesus was restoring my self-esteem.

Mike, who was the pastor at that time, would ask people every few weeks whether they wanted to become a Christian if they hadn't done so already. He asked everyone to close their eyes and then he invited people who wanted to become Christians to open their eyes and look at him so that he would know and could talk to them after. It wasn't hyped up or loud, but really peaceful. Without a second thought, I opened my eyes and stared directly at him because I wanted him to know about the commitment I'd made with Julie a few weeks before. I knew that life had been so tough but God was for me and he could help me even though I had been so full of anger, pain and disappointment. I felt such peace that I can't explain and the peace just kept growing and growing and growing, the more I spent time with God. All the anger and trauma and fear had been wiped away and I stood as a new person.

After the service, I wanted to talk to Jimmy about what I'd done. 'Jimmy,' I said, 'when Mike asked people to look at him if they wanted to become Christians…well…I looked at him.' My heart almost stopped whilst I waited for Jimmy's response. Jimmy turned round with a look of pure joy on his face and said, 'I did too. I looked at Mike too!' It was incredible. We'd never been united before we became Christians. Our marriage had been like a struggle for survival, but now there was something that brought us together. Mike came to talk to us after the service about our commitment to Jesus and offered us a book to read. 'I've already got that one,' I said with happiness. 'Julie lent it to me!' 'Well,' said Mike 'It looks like there's nothing else I need to talk to you about. Sounds like Julie is really looking after you very well.'

My whole life completely changed when I met Jesus. He took all my anger away and softened my heart. I stopped swearing, but not because I tried really hard to. I just stopped. It was as simple as that. God was changing me from the inside out. Friends and family remarked about how much I'd changed and Jimmy and I were overjoyed when we were baptised together at the church. It was amazing to see where there had been so much tension and worry between us that God had brought us into relationship with him together, taken us to church together and also baptised us together. It was amazing. I never dreamed that my life would turn around so much. My friends and family came to the church when we were baptised too, which was incredible as I wanted them to see how God had changed our lives. They were so impacted by what they heard.

Since then, I have started volunteering for CAP too and it's such a joy to help people who are in a similar situation to what I was. When God heals you, it makes you want to share that with other people. Going on visits with Julie enables me to support people as I understand what it's like to face the trauma of debt.

It's a Tuesday night and I'm about to go out. Jimmy is inside watching the TV and relaxing on the sofa. It's amazing to be surrounded by people that love and care for me and my social life is well and truly alive! It's so great to wave goodbye to all those threatening calls from the bank and also the letters. We don't get many through the post now and when we do, it's straight in an envelope with them and up to CAP's head office. I don't have to fear the post arriving any more and because I'm eating properly on our new budget, my diabetes is under control.

With the new financial plan, I can afford a little luxury every now and then, as Jimmy and I pay off the debt. Tonight the treat is a Chinese meal round at a friend's house from church. I can't wait. I feel such peace now. Looking back at how angry I was, I can't believe I survived for so long. God has taken all that, though.

Suddenly, there's a knock at the door but the fear I used to feel has gone. No worries about doorstep debt collectors now. That's all gone, swept away and placed firmly in the past. I open the door. 'Hi,' I say to my friend 'I'll be out in a minute,' and I put my coat on. I peer round the lounge door and see my husband, on the sofa. 'Jimmy, my friends are here. I'm going out now. I'll be back about ten.' 'Ok, I'll see you later,' he replies 'and make sure you have a great time.'

'I will,' I say to him with fondness. I turn towards the front door to leave, but turn around again to face him. 'One more thing, Jimmy,' I say. 'What's that?' he replies.

'I love you.'

3. BRIGHT FUTURE

Lloyd's Story

I've been break-dancing for a while now and my aim is to be the best in the world in a few years' time. At the moment, I've got my eyes on a competition in Las Vegas and it's the World Championships. It's a fantastic opportunity. I'm teaching breakdance in schools too, with arguably the best female breakdancer in the world. It's such a privilege and I never dreamed I'd be able to do this. It's amazing how much things have changed. Sometimes I feel like I'm living someone else's life. I look at myself and all the opportunities I have and wonder how I got here. I can buy clothes when I need now, have savings in the bank and I'm earning good money.

I've not always had it so easy though. I was born in Bradford in 1986 and the city was really different to how it is now. There was a lot more poverty I think and people found it really hard to make ends meet. It was the same in my family. Looking back, I know there must have been money issues, because we moved all the time. I think we moved eight times in total.

West Bowling, Allerton, Whetley Hill …We live in East Bowling now, which is a really nice area. We've lived here for the past four years, but we did move around a lot and often lived in bad neighbourhoods.

It's sometimes hard for me to remember that far back. Mum worked night shifts as a nurse in different hospitals across the city and at one point owned a driving school with my dad. The school failed and it pushed them to financial breaking point and into uncontrollable debt. To try and get out of the debt, Mum worked as many hours as possible to pay the interest we owed and to make sure we ate.

I can't really remember seeing Mum much when I was young, but I do remember her wearing a nurse's uniform and then going out of the house to work. You know how you can just remember small glimpses of people as they rush in and out of your life. It was like that with Mum. I have these vague memories of her being there in her uniform, then in the next instance, gone. At the time it seemed normal. I didn't really understand what was happening, but looking back I know it must have been awful for her not to be around when we were growing up and it wasn't easy for me and my brother too.

Food was another thing that made me realise we were really short of money. We ate the same food all the time. One of the main things we ate was dumplings and beans. Dad is West Indian, so dumplings aren't uncommon in Caribbean food, but often that was the only thing we got to eat. It was the dumplings or corned beef, corned beef or dumplings. We would also have cornmeal to fill us up, which I hated.

I'd never eat those things again. I hated that cornmeal stuff we had to eat and I couldn't stand corned beef either. It was cheap food and there was no variety. It was all we ate, day after day, week after week. I guess it was because there was literally no money.

When I was younger, I had a tall and skinny frame. I would injure myself all the time when breakdancing. Bones, muscles, the whole thing. I seemed to be injured constantly. I just had no strength...

Clothes were another thing that made me realise we were really hard up. Like the food, there was never any variety. We'd wear the same thing again and again, until we'd worn it out. As a child I rarely had new clothes. Mum got really angry once because my brother put his knee through his new school trousers on the first day of school. I guess that was a sign that we couldn't afford another pair.

That's the thing about being in poverty through debt; it robs you of variety. Things were relentless; the food, the clothes, the house moves. It was the repetitive nature of it all that made it so relentless.

It was the lack of money that pushed me towards breakdancing. It costs nothing to do. When I first started, I'd practice by myself for hours and hours. There was no-one else; just me and the opportunity to become the best I possibly could. There was no other option for entertainment. With the financial difficulties, I can't remember when we went out on trips as a family. It was hard enough for Mum to feed us, let alone pay for trips to the cinema and meals out. After a few years of practising by myself, I finally met up with some other breakdancers and it took me by surprise how much more I was able to improve.

The thing is, just as stuff was really taking off with the breakdancing, things got really bad at home. I can remember clearly how money became even scarcer just before Mum and Dad split up. I think the pressure of it all must have been immense. It must have been so hard. A few years previously, Mum had approached John Kirkby at CAP and he'd worked hard to try to sort our finances out. Things had stabilised until around the time of the split, but when Mum and Dad broke up, Mum couldn't afford to pay back the debts any more. It was devastating for her, but she had to declare herself bankrupt. I can't imagine the disappointment she must have felt, having tried for so long to keep it all together.

It was a tough time for all of us. Money was tighter than ever, the divorce broke Mum and we moved to a rougher area of town. Just the three of us; Mum, me and my brother. Another move, another neighbourhood. Luckily I managed to stay in the same school, which was precious stability in the midst of all the change.

I remember quite vividly how we moved to a new housing estate. It hadn't been built very long, but you could tell there was real poverty there. Things were hard for everyone. It was full of new buildings, but you could tell that in a few years time, it would all go downhill like the other estates in the city. Our house had those bars on the windows. You could tell people had low expectations of how the neighbourhood would turn out. The bars said it all, really. It was hard to tell if they were there to stop people breaking in or to trap the residents in this hopeless estate. This was rock-bottom for us. We'd been through so much and I think Mum wondered about when it was all going to end.

For my mum, the bankruptcy cleared her debts and meant she could start afresh. As for me, I continued to breakdance and reached a level where I could teach and earn a wage from it too. That meant I was able to save. I've always set targets for myself with saving. At first, I wanted to have fifty pounds in the bank, then one hundred, then five hundred. Money gives you options. Now I have options but I never waste money. Seeing the torment that Mum went through, I never want to get into debt myself.

My mum was John Kirkby's second ever client, a fore-runner for all the people that would be helped through CAP. Seeing my mum go through what she went through really made me not want to get into debt myself. My life has really changed dramatically

I really love eating out in restaurants now. Whereas paying for food used to be a daily struggle for Mum and we had to eat the same food day in, day out, now I can pick and choose where I want dinner. It's nice to be able to buy clothes when I'd like as well. Looking back over those times when I had so few clothes, it makes me grateful that Mum got help and got us out of that situation. As a family, we've said goodbye to constant house moves, window bars and living in fear. I pray we've said goodbye to debt too, forever. That's one life I never want to return to.

A Mother's Perspective:

Lloyd and I have just come back from a fantastic three-day holiday in the Lakes to celebrate his twenty-first birthday. Our relationship has changed so much over the years and we're busy making up for lost time now. Before I had children, I'd always dreamed about being a stay-at-home mum, building a family and cherishing each moment as the kids grew up. I was desperately sad to be forced into work whilst they were still so young. Lloyd was three years old at the time when I started working night shifts to make ends meet.

It was a difficult time and even when I was around at home, my thoughts were on catching up on lost sleep and whether I'd be able to survive the next gruelling, eleven-hour shift.

For the past five years, since I've been debt free, I've had a continual focus on the kids. Well, young adults I should say now. There's barely a week that goes by when Lloyd and I don't go out for some food. We love going to a café or a restaurant and catching up, eating and drinking, enjoying one another's company. We've got the freedom to do that now and have options available to us. Sadly, when Lloyd and his brother were growing up, options and freedom were two things we could not afford.

Everything was a struggle, just to get through daily life was hard – right from being three to thirteen Lloyd was caught up in this and suffered a lot. My divorce went through and I declared myself bankrupt all in the space of a few months. It was a devastating time. It was rock bottom for us. Moving onto that estate made me cry out to God. I wondered where it was all going to end, where we would end up, how we could ever escape this hopeless neighbourhood. My youngest son didn't leave the house for the first two years that we lived there. He simply went to school, came home and stayed indoors. It was not living but existing. It was so demoralising for us all. Still, you keep praying, keep holding on to God, keep trusting for his miracles.

It was at this time that Lloyd became involved with a breakdancing group at our new church. They were such a close-knit bunch of people. I remember Lloyd observing for a year or so before he plucked up the courage to go and join in. At that time, he had so little self-confidence. I guess life took that out of him at a painfully young age and it was only through God that he reclaimed it.

The leaders of that group really loved and supported Lloyd and nurtured this fledgling talent too. They didn't always go easy on him, but I think he recognised how much potential they saw in him and they didn't want him to settle for second best. If I was to use one word to describe Lloyd, it's potential. I'm convinced he has the potential to do whatever he wants. Breakdancing is just the tip of the iceberg. I go to see him perform sometimes and I'm amazed at what he can do. I stand there and think about my young son, my son who had so little when he was growing up and think about how his life has changed. I feel so proud.

4. TRANSFORMATION

Ralph's Story

It's Sunday morning. I've just woken up. All I can think about is the complete financial mess I have got into – I can't switch it off. Why can't I get rid of all the thoughts crowding my mind? I get out of bed and my stomach is in a knot, my body is tingling and my brain is not functioning. All these silly thoughts of topping myself fill my head – after all I have nowt to live for. I need to brush my teeth, but put a cigarette in my mouth instead. Stumbling, I get dressed, eat a bit of breakfast and head off to the pub across the way. Sitting in the pub I drink my first pint. A few pints later I wander back home and fall asleep – ready for my next session at the pub.

I'm sixty-seven and was born and bred here in Edmonsey. As a family we didn't have much and drinking simply became a way of life for me. We lived in a four bedroom house, with no hot running water and a toilet we had to share with the neighbours. It was a rough upbringing, but pleasant. I wasn't the brightest kid at school. My teachers called me 'a dull star', but I liked football, cricket, gardening, arithmetic and history. I loved singing!

My mum said I was rotten to the core and I believed her. I used to go out drinking with all the lads in the village, just to prove that I could. We'd have a drinking session in the afternoon where I'd down at least fourteen pints. The pub was just next door, so I didn't have far to go! After a short break to sleep off some of the alcohol, I'd return to the pub for the evening drinks – again another fourteen pints was the norm. It was then that the fights would start. I got into some real big fights. We used to have 'student bashing nights'. Me, my brother and some mates would go to this pub called 'The Big Jug' in Durham. We'd drink some pints and then look for targets. It was usually the 'la-di-dah' posh students we'd attack. We'd shout obscenities at them and just goad them until they retaliated, which they usually did. I was a good fighter and eight out of ten times we'd win! This was the routine every night I could. It was the culture you see. I had to prove myself to my 'mates'.

Boy was I bad. I did many things that I now regret. I was violent and used that violence whenever someone did something to upset me. When kids came round the house asking for tuppence I would just shout at them and reach through the letter box and pull their hair. I didn't want them bothering me.

I hated cats – absolutely hated them! One day me and one of the lads found these cats and shoved them in an oil drum at a local garage. We poured in oil and water, shook it around a bit and then lit some gas. The drum exploded, cats and all. I got some stick for that little stunt, I can tell you. I'm ashamed of it now, but at the time, that was who I was.

All the drinking took such a toll on my body. I weighed only nine and a half stone – I wasn't eating properly and just drank as much as possible. In 1988, I was diagnosed with diabetes and told to stop drinking. In a way, this was the wake up call I needed. I stopped drinking (as much!) just like that. I didn't have any withdrawal symptoms. I cut back gradually and now only drink two or three pints a time. I don't really know how I did it – I just stopped. I suppose I didn't feel that pressure any more, the diabetes gave me a way out of that culture. I continued to go the pub and have fun with the lads, but just didn't drink as much.

My life continued in the same routine, but I had a series of jobs along the way. My first job was in an office when I was just sixteen. Believe it or not I was very bashful and shy. I then went and worked on a dairy farm for two years, before moving to a bakery and then becoming a scaffolder. I then settled down as a Refuge Disposal Officer or bin man. I did that for twenty-five years. I hated it, but it put money on the table. I'd carry the bins on my shoulders, stinking water would pour down my back and litter would go everywhere. My mother said I stunk. She would force me into the bath as soon as I got in.

So life went on. I almost got married, but it didn't work out, so I lived with my mother and father until they died. Up until that point my finances were fine.

It was after I had been living on my own for two or three years that the problems with my finances began. When I got my electricity bill, I was convinced that I should be paying more, so I phoned them up, but they kept telling me that everything was fine and I was paying the right amount. Each time I phoned they told me the same thing – so I believed them.

One day I got this letter from the company saying that I owed them £1,440 and that they wanted £104 per month to pay the debt. I couldn't believe it. I didn't understand how they could get it so wrong. I felt frustrated because I knew that I had used the electricity and would have to pay for it, but because of their error I was landed with this huge debt.

I had other debts that I could manage, but this electricity bill was the tipping point. I simply couldn't afford it. It was then that the other debts began to snowball out of control. Every bill was getting more and more and I just felt lost. I did not know what to do or where to turn. I just couldn't afford to live.

Have you ever had that experience where you are really nervous about going somewhere and that's all you can think about? Your stomach churns and you just want it all to be over. Well, that's what I felt everyday. I was plagued with suicidal thoughts and would cry all the time. I couldn't eat because of the stress and was just getting more and more depressed. I didn't have a clue which way to turn.

It was suggested that I go to Age Concern because I just didn't know what to do. I took all my bills to them and when one of the lads saw them he said, 'You need CAP'. That evening I had a message from Janet (Durham Centre Manager). She seemed alright and arranged to come and see me that week.

So Janet arrived, bustling into my living room with a kind look on her face. She brought a lady called Angela with her. She came in, introduced herself and asked to see all my bills. I gave them to her and she said she'd sort it out. Then she asked me if I wanted to pray. I didn't believe in God, but thought 'if it makes her feel good then I will.'

After that first meeting Angela took me to the supermarket as I didn't have much food in the house. She bought me £60 worth of groceries. Well, I was gobsmacked, shocked and completely overwhelmed! I was chuffed to bits! I couldn't believe that anyone would actually do that for me, a man that believed he was rotten to the core and not worth a thing. It was then that I began to believe that there were humane people on the planet – not just rotten people like me. I started to think, 'maybe there's a God after all.'

Janet's office is based in a charity shop run by her church, so I went to meet her there. When I walked in I saw this lady, Joan, standing there. There was something different about her. She was so warm, calm and relaxed. It was strange. I was thinking, 'Where the heck am I?' I asked her what the shop was and she explained that it was a charity shop that sells clothes to raise money for India and Albania – church projects. I said I was looking for Janet and she took me upstairs for our meeting.

She had gone through my finances and sorted out how much I needed to pay into my CAP Account. I must confess I was a little scared at first. But once I knew the road I was on, everything felt smooth.

I began to trust what Janet was doing. I don't open any mail that comes in, as it just freaks me out, instead I send everything to CAP. It's great.

Because of my experience with Janet, Joan and Angela I thought I'd try their church just to see what it was like. My friend Muriel already went to the church and there was a special minibus that they used to pick people up from my village because the buses didn't operate at the right times for church.

Muriel is now my best-friend. She is also a CAP client and lives in my village. I knew her and saw her around but we weren't close. I got to know Muriel better through CAP and the events the centre organised, so working with CAP also gave me a great friend.

My first impression was that it was a beautiful church with beautiful people. I thought there was an amazing atmosphere. People were actually speaking to each other – and seemed to really care about each other! I hadn't known people like that and couldn't believe it. They were just so different. The leader, Alan, blessed me – even though it was the first time he had ever seen me.

I really enjoyed the singing although I didn't know the words! During the service, I really sensed God's love. It was like this warm feeling going up my back – I could have cried, it was just so incredible. It was so strange. I felt like there was something there that just wanted to pick up the pieces of my life. I heard this voice saying, 'I'm here if you need me. I will pick up the pieces. I will put you on the right side of the path – but you've got to make that decision and help yourself.' I then decided to put my whole heart and soul into belief in God and at that point I became a Christian. I went to Alan after the service and said that I wanted to get baptised there and then, and asked Muriel if I could come back next Sunday!

I didn't get baptised that day, but waited until November 2007. It was amazing! Muriel baptised me with Alan. She said it was a hoot, and threatened to drown me! But I knew just how pleased and proud she was! The water was so cold. I felt like an iceberg on the outside, but inside I was just bursting with warmth! When I was pulled up from the water, I was tingling all over. But this time it was a good tingly feeling, not like the dark days before CAP.

I am now a member of the church. I was chuffed to bits when I was welcomed into the membership – I could barely contain my happiness! I go to a men's cell group every week and a prayer breakfast once a month. I just love my church; I love the singing and I love the people. My favourite song is 'Lord you have my Heart.' I love and respect God and I love and respect Jesus. My life is completely transformed. I am in another world.

I went on a holiday with CAP last Christmas. Whilst I had a great time, I actually felt homesick for church! Who would have thought it!

Another incredible thing is that I've experienced healing. I used to have arthritis in my knee. At the end of one of the services, there was some prayer for healing. This great little lass, Julie, came up to me and said, 'Why aren't you up there?' So, I went up and one of the elders was there. I said, 'I want prayer for this daft knee.' He put his hand on my knee. I prayed saying, 'This time Gaffer.' That's my name for God. As the elder's hand was on my knee, it felt warm – even when he took away his hand. It stayed warm for the next five minutes. When that warmth went, I was healed! I couldn't believe it. I had to keep checking I was healed for about a week after! When I went to the doctor's I told him I didn't need the painkillers any more because I was healed. He was very doubtful but, lo and behold, it was true! I was so happy!

I've changed in more ways than just being healed. I used to be racist – but not any more. I used to look at people with contempt, thinking 'this is my England', but I don't now. I call them brothers. They are my friends. I shake hands with people and hug them. I am also more generous – too generous apparently! I even give little treats to the kids that come round. I am stronger in myself. I know where my heart is and while I have a lot to learn, I just hope God is pleased with me.

I also love animals now! I'm perfectly content to sit in my best friend Muriel's house surrounded by rabbits, dogs and cats. I've no desire to harm them and actually enjoy their presence.

Muriel tells me that I beam now! That my face is different. She says I used to look 'grey', but now my eyes are so different and my face doesn't look twisted with bitterness. I have a much better self-image. She tells people that I'm the world's best evangelist, but in the most cock-eyed manner!

It's true though. I always talk about what God has done and how great the church is. I don't care who I tell. CAP has given me a new life, a new look at life, a reason to be happy and a reason to be glad. I pray to God every night and thank him for what he's done.'

It's Sunday morning. I've just woken up. I feel at peace. I get up, have a bath, eat breakfast and go round to Muriel's. I catch the bus to church and have a great time singing to God. I then go round to Joan's, and the three of us have lunch. No pain, no stress – just peace and laughter. My life is transformed and CAP has saved my life.

Ralph's story ends with Dan, Ralph's Caseworker in our Client Support Unit telling him that his last payment to the bank has just been paid. He is now debt-free. Ralph looks slightly stunned and whispers to Dan, 'Thank you – you have saved my life, but can I keep working with CAP even now I'm debt-free?' Dan replies, 'Of course you can' and Ralph smiles a relieved smile. I realise that CAP is not about just the here and now. It's about the future – setting people free to live the life that God has intended for them.

Susan & Paul

5. WHOLENESS

Susan's Story

'Just eat it, there's not much.' 'Come on, just try a small bit, I'm sure you'll like it.' 'Please eat, I beg you, you're making yourself ill.' 'Can't you see what you are doing – do you want to die?' 'Why are you doing this to us, can't you see the effect it is having?' 'Don't you care about us?'

You think it's easy. All you have to do is pick up the knife and fork, put the food in your mouth, start chewing and swallow. But it isn't. Something inside me is repelled by food. My body tells me that if I continue not to eat I will die, but my head doesn't agree. My hair is falling out, I've lost all my teeth and can no longer grow my nails, but still I can't break the habit. My son keeps telling me of all the research he's been doing on the internet. He tells me of a woman who died because of the illness we know of as anorexia. But it doesn't make any difference. I can't get out of this prison. I can't eat. I'm past the point of hunger now.

I've been anorexic ever since I was sixteen. At school I was pleasantly plump, but it didn't bother me as I was content in who I was. However, school can be so cruel, especially when it's an all girl grammar school. Some of the girls were so nasty. They called me every name under the sun and would draw pictures of me on the blackboard. I only had one friend, Karen.

When I was thirteen, I saw a boy called Tony. I fell for him instantly. Karen and I used to sit on the wall watching him play football. I found out everything I could about him, his name, age, likes and dislikes. Eventually he noticed me and asked me out. He was so great!

The girls at school couldn't believe that 'fatty' had a boyfriend, so Tony used to come and meet me after school. The girls still didn't believe me and eventually my best friend Karen joined their gang. I had no-one at school, but I didn't care as I had Tony and my family.

When I was sixteen, Tony proposed and I couldn't have been happier. I was engaged to a wonderful guy, life was good.

My world fell apart when I received a random call from Tony. I remember that day vividly. He phoned and just said he couldn't see me any more and could I go round and collect my stuff. When I arrived at his house, he was standing at his front door with all my things. I didn't understand, I begged him to give me a reason, but he refused. He said he couldn't tell me why and just said bye.

I was absolutely devastated. I didn't understand. What was wrong with me? Was I too fat?

It was at that point that I stopped eating. I decided that if I was thin then I would easily get another boyfriend and be accepted by the girls at school. When I met the father of my first child Lucy*, my anorexia wasn't an issue for him. He just allowed me to continue in it and never challenged me.

To be honest, the anorexia came in phases. If something good happened and I was happy I would eat a little, but it wouldn't last for long. It only took the smallest thing to set me back again. At my worst, I got down to six stone two pounds.

Lucy's father left me a few years after her birth, and I was left as a single parent. I met Paul in 1983 when Lucy was four. He was at my neighbour's house when I dropped her off one day. It was really sweet, he asked my neighbour for permission to ask me out! As he was only nineteen and I was twenty-five, I was a bit unsure. But he had a motorbike, so that won it over for me!

We arranged to meet the following Saturday. He still lived at home and when I came round he was hiding in the kitchen and wouldn't come out! Apparently he was just so shocked that I'd actually said yes! He said I was so pretty that he'd expected me to reject him!

However, he did venture out of the house and we had a great day. It was love at first sight! I'd only known him a short time, but I knew he was 'the one'. It was like a story book – our eyes met and that was it. That was in the January, and we were married in May! We had our first son George* in 1984, followed by Katie* two years later.

When I first met Paul I was so happy that I was in a phase of eating a little. But things soon began to revert back and I was drinking but not eating. Paul could see what was going on, but I was in denial. It took the birth of my daughter Katie to make me try and do something about it. I was only seven stone three when I had Katie. The midwife was in shock. She couldn't believe that I had been allowed to give birth.

After Katie's birth, I went to see a psychologist. She told me that if I got a job, then I would feel a lot better and it would help me move on from my anorexia. If only it was that simple. I got a job as a waitress in a local hotel. I worked in the conference and banqueting side of the hotel, so was confronted each day with food. You might think that being around food would tempt me back into eating, but conversely it provided me with the ideal opportunity of hiding my problem.

All the staff would spend the day grazing on the food and they just thought I was strong-willed and didn't like to eat much. This meant I didn't get any pressure from them there – not a good thing really. I had believed my psychologist when she said working would help and I was so disappointed when it had the opposite effect. I felt so let down. I had really hoped the job would change me – but it hadn't.

Life continued to be a struggle and eventually I came to a point when I wanted out. I felt like I was on a rollercoaster. Everything was going so fast and I needed to get off it. Paul's family also interfered a lot in our relationship. They would discuss my life and it was like going to court. I felt like I was suffocating. I still loved Paul, but it was all too much. It wasn't Paul I was divorcing, it was the situation. I wanted his family's support, but I needed them to let us deal with our problems on our own.

However, we couldn't stay away from each other for long. In less than a year we were seeing each other again. I was a bit scared and dubious about seeing him again, but I loved him so much. We actually saw more of each other during that time than we had when we were together! It wasn't long before Paul moved back in. In 1994, I gave birth to Ben* and then in 1997 James* was born. In 2000, we bought our first house together. It was an ex-Council house and we bought it at a great price.

Then, on 22 September 2005, we got re-married. It was a quiet affair, just me, Paul, my sister, my daughter Katie and the two youngest boys. We married at a registry office in Scarborough because we'd had great holidays there. It was really special. The registry office provided two cushions for the boys to carry the rings on. Our first wedding had been too big and extravagant for our liking, so to have something small was lovely.

Little did I know back in 2000 when we bought our house, just what a trap we had fallen into. At the time we were amazed by how cheap it was and were so happy to have our own house. After all, I was a waitress and Paul a forklift truck driver, so it was amazing that we could even get on the property ladder. Cosmetically the house had looked great, but under the surface it was a disaster waiting to happen.

---

*Name changed to protect identity

The entire house needed re-plastering and re-wiring, and the costs snowballed. We needed to make the house habitable. So, we took on a second mortgage on the house to pay off our debts and finish all the work. Although we could maintain the payments for a few years, we hadn't thought about long-term implications. Paul had been in his job since he was sixteen and I was now working at a supermarket.

But then, on 21 June 2007, the bottom fell out of my world – Paul was made redundant. He'd been there twenty-eight years and it came like a bolt out of the blue. He'd had a letter saying that he was in a high-risk category, but had been told his job was secure. We were devastated.

It was the final straw. Our mortgage was extortionate, as were the repayments on our secured loan. We were paying over £1,000 per month. It was just too much. We knew we were in major trouble and would certainly lose the house if Paul didn't get another job.

Mentally and emotionally I just fell apart. I still struggled with anorexia, an emergency blood transfusion for chronic anaemia couldn't stop the habit, and these debts didn't do anything to help. I felt like a complete failure.

Not only was I causing pain to my entire family because of my anorexia, I couldn't even keep a roof over my children's heads as we were facing eviction. The central heating had broken on Christmas Day 2007, so I couldn't even keep them warm. I can't tell you the hurt and agony it is to feel like you've let your family down. My children have never been spoilt with the latest gadgets etc, but to not be able to give them even the basics was absolutely heartbreaking.

My bedroom became my safe-haven. It was a struggle even to see the children. I didn't want to see anyone. I would look in the mirror and didn't recognise the person looking out. The person with fight and positivity had gone. I was replaced by a broken woman, sad and defeated. All the doors had shut. I was in a long dark tunnel with no end in sight. I felt like they would all be much better off without me.

I was off work for three months. Once I had given the children their breakfast and sent them off to school, and Paul had gone to college to do the course recommended by the Job Centre, I would get dressed and sit on my bed. I didn't want to be at home, but couldn't go out either. I didn't even watch TV. I didn't read. I just sat there staring into space thinking about how my life was deteriorating before my very eyes.

My 'other self' was a nasty one, full of anger. I would lose my temper really easily. Paul has been through some horrendous times with me. In my real lows I would bombard him with hate. I would blame him for being made redundant, for buying the house and anything else I could attack him for. I have also said things to the children that I will never forgive myself for saying. To prevent this I would sit in my room fighting against this new me, which I labelled 'hate'. It was absolutely exhausting.

Poor Paul was also in similar turmoil. He felt like he'd let the family down by not having a job, and was angry, frustrated and depressed. It was so hard for him. All he'd known was working in a factory. He hadn't even wanted to go into factory work, but had been forced to by his parents. This meant that he didn't have any other skills.

In the meantime, the debt kept getting worse and worse as we couldn't meet our repayments. The phone calls, the post – it was never ending. We simply did not know where to turn.

Our saving grace came in the form of Christians Against Poverty. Our youngest son has learning difficulties so we have a Social Service worker. She had heard of CAP, but didn't really know what they did. So in February 2008, I made the phone call. I spoke to a man called Chris. He asked me some basic background information and arranged a visit to see us.

Chris managed to get a financial statement in place to get the creditors off our backs so we could deal with the impending repossession of our house. He even came to court with us on 2 April and we got an extension of fifty-six days. An eviction date was set for 28 May, but we are still in the property! Whilst we know that eventually we will be evicted, because of CAP's amazing system, we are building up savings. When 'D-day' does come round, we will have enough saved to provide a deposit and the first month's rent on a new house. I know that CAP will support us every step of the way.

The amazing thing is that if you had told me a few months earlier that I would be waiting to be evicted with no idea where we will live, I would have completely freaked out. Yet, we aren't worried about the future. We don't just focus on the negatives any more, we know there will be a solution. The reason for this peace has not only been because of input from CAP, but because of meeting Jesus.

Unbeknown to us, Chris had nominated us for a holiday with CAP. We couldn't believe it. I hadn't had a holiday for years. I was back at work by then and strangely, my supervisor had pencilled in holiday for me on the same week as the break. Even though Paul's college initially refused him time off, after some pleading from me about what the holiday was and how much we needed it, they gave Paul permission to go. It had all slotted into place as it was meant to be. I even got my daughter Katie to look after our dog, Angel.

We weren't sure what to expect and I was nervous about the eating side of the holiday. I still struggled with anorexia and wasn't sure whether we'd all eat together or separately, and how I'd be able to avoid it. On the way to the holiday, Chris told us that we'd arrive just in time for lunch. Alarm bells instantly went off and I started sweating. I was so scared and unsure.

When we got there we went and unpacked and then went to meet Chris for lunch. The lunch was to be served by waitresses and we were all to eat together. We sat down and some fish and chips arrived in front of me. I sat there talking to Chris and another CAP staff member, Andy. Before I knew it I'd eaten all the lunch – it was gone! I even ate dessert, mixed fruit and ice cream.

From that day on, I sat down and ate three meals a day with my family and other clients – a main and a pudding. I was bursting at the seams! It even got to the stage that I was looking forward to going to meals. I would look at my watch and tell the family how long it was before dinner. I was the one who wanted to go and eat. Nothing negative entered my head. There was just such an air of peace and tranquillity throughout the whole place.

I suppose I knew no-one would judge me if I didn't eat the food, it would just be taken away. This meant I didn't feel pressurised to eat and it actually became the most normal thing to do despite years struggling to eat even one meal.

Paul was over the moon. He didn't say anything and make a big thing of it though because he wanted it to become natural, normal. He's so proud of me – as are our children. However, he was scared that I would revert back as soon as we came home.

That holiday was a turning point and was the biggest thing to happen in my life, especially when I found God. There were meetings that we could go to if we wanted. We were wary, but went along anyway. During one meeting they showed the NOOMA DVD

'Rain' by Rob Bell. As we watched it, it really connected to me. Before, every day had felt like a rainy day and I couldn't see the sunshine, even when it was sunny. After watching the film we had a chat to Josie Barlow (a CAP staff member) about God. We learnt about what it was to be a Christian and how God could bring peace into your life, despite any outside circumstances. So we both decided to give our hearts to God. It was amazing – we both felt so at peace.

Our two youngest sons, Ben and James, were impacted by the holiday too. Before we went, they couldn't stand each other. They were always fighting, with Ben taking out a lot of frustration on James. It was so upsetting especially as they were brothers. Yet, during the break, something changed inside them. They actually started having fun with each other. We found we were able to let them play table tennis or football, without us needing to be there to supervise. This was great for me and Paul. We had time to ourselves to be a real couple, without worrying about the boys hurting each other. It was also wonderful to then sit down for dinner as a family.

All of us have changed because of CAP and God. We will often go for a walk and sometimes get caught out by the rain. Instead of moaning and becoming grumpy, we just laugh.

Before all my problems, I was known as a smiler! I love people and love making them laugh. Before going away with CAP, that person had disappeared, but now she's back and raring to go! I smile all the time now. Whilst life is not without its challenges, I know I can face it.

I am still battling with my eating, but it feels so different. I sit down for an evening meal with Paul, and some nights we have dinner as a family. Sundays are now set aside for the family. We sit down for Sunday dinner and we talk. Even Ben, my fourteen year old talks. He has had Attention Deficit Hyperactivity Disorder since he was five.

I can now talk to him without him getting angry. He even apologised at school when he was naughty and was allowed to stay in the lesson. This is a miracle. Ben has had twenty-five incidents at school since September 2007 alone.

Ben and James continue to get on well. The play a lot together and Ben is breaking away from the boys who've had such a bad influence in his life. He even asks James if he can play with him and his friends.

Paul is also a new person. People used to call him 'my shadow'. He just wouldn't go anywhere without me, as he couldn't face people on his own. I was the outgoing one and Paul would just sit in a corner. It was certainly a case of opposites attract! But now he's got a new outlook on life. He even went and joined the local library on his own. He wants another job that requires using his brain and working with people. He now stands up for himself and is over-flowing with confidence.

Paul and I have been through so much. I wouldn't be without him. We've overcome many, many challenges and ridden many storms, but because of CAP and God we are much stronger as a family. We know God has a plan for us. We know he won't let us down and we will continue to have a happy home, whatever the future.

Phil, Zoe and their three children

6. REVELATION

Phil and Zoe's Story

Strange that there's a letter addressed to me in the post, I think to myself, as I struggle across the doormat and make my way through to the kitchen with the heavy bags of shopping. Zoe's right behind me as we negotiate the kids' toys on the floor following what feels like a mammoth supermarket shop. 'I wasn't expecting any post today' I say to her, but she doesn't seem to have any idea who it's from either. I leave the bags on the work-surface in the kitchen and go back to the doormat.

Picking up the letter I take it into the kitchen, where Zoe, my beautiful wife, is already unpacking the shopping. Our two kids are in the living room, watching Saturday morning TV and Zoe's glowing; we've just found out we're expecting our third child and I couldn't be happier. I've a great job that pays well, a fantastic house, two wonderful kids and an amazing wife. Life doesn't get any better than this, I think to myself. I couldn't ask for anything else.

'Who's that letter from?' Zoe asks. I tell her I don't know and start to open the envelope. Zoe stops her unpacking and stands next to me, looking over my shoulder to see who it's from. I take the letter out and unfold it. It's from my main contractor. I'm an independent IT consultant and I've worked for this company for quite a few years and they pay great. So great in fact, that we've been able to afford the odd holiday, good cars and this beautiful house. Yeah, it's all bought on credit, but who cares? I know we can always pay it back. Then it happens.

'Phil', says Zoe, her voice trembling 'What's this about your contract ending?'

My heart stops.

I've not read that far down the letter yet, but as I tumble through the sentences, reality starts to hit home. Four weeks of work left.

No job after that. Main contractor is terminating my contract. 'What?' I say to Zoe, poring over the letter to see if we've read it wrong. 'I don't believe it.' Zoe has gone quiet by this point, but her hand still rests on my shoulder. I read the letter through a third time, hoping I've made a mistake but the words just won't change. Zoe is still silent, but already I'm trying to put a brave face on it in spite of the shock. 'I'm sure I'll find something else, darling,' I say, but I'm struggling to understand why it has happened.

I knew the company was looking to streamline things a little, but I had no idea that they'd be getting rid of me. After all, I've put my heart and soul into that company; blood, sweat and tears and all that. Late nights and early mornings and working round the clock. Yeah, they paid well, but I certainly earned my keep.

'Zoe, I'll get other work,' I say, but she's silent. Then the shock hits me. My hands start to shake and trembling, I put the letter back on the work-surface. I've got no job, I suddenly realise; no way of supporting the family unless I find more work in the next four weeks. No way of affording the mortgage. No way of paying back the finance deal on the car. No way of paying back the other loan I took out. No way of paying for food...I suddenly snap myself out of it though, as I'm starting to think the worst. Everything's going to be OK, I say to myself, in a bid for self-assurance. Zoe turns me round to hug me and lets out a sigh.

'I love you. I'm so sorry, but please don't worry. You're going to find other work,' she says, but by this point, I'm barely listening; I'm focussed on where I can find another contract in the next four weeks before we stop having any income at all. 'I love you too, darling and you're right, I will find other work,' I say, but it's like the words just tumble out automatically, as if someone else is saying them for me.

I first met Zoe when we were teenagers and part of the same church youth group. She was my first love and our relationship survived those awkward years when so many other couples seemed to break up. She always believed in God as had I when we first met, but things started to change when I went to college. I'd always been interested in creation and geology and the history of the earth and I got into problems when I took an intellectual approach to my faith. I just couldn't work things out in my head and the God of the Bible didn't seem to fit in with what I was reading about the earth and how it came about and the age of rocks and other things that I'd studied.

Like the rocks, my faith got eroded little by little over the space of a few years. It was nothing major at first; just a little doubt about something, but I think it created weak spots in my faith and as time went by, the cracks just got wider. Before I realised it, there wasn't much left. 'So much for God', I thought to myself; I could do things fine myself. I'd let Zoe be the 'Bible-basher' in our relationship.

When I was twenty-three and Zoe was twenty, we got married. We were overjoyed. It was such a happy occasion. At the time Zoe was still studying and I wasn't earning much, so my mum very kindly agreed to re-mortgage her house to help us get a foot on the property ladder. It was such a kind gesture and one we really appreciated at the time. Zoe and I moved into a flat; our first home together and things were looking very promising for the future. Then, things got even better when we found out that Zoe was expecting our first child. We were so happy at the time. I was really looking forward to being a dad and supporting our family; my wage was growing all the time and although we lost out because the property market had dropped, we moved to a bigger house in expectation of our new arrival.

After a couple of years we thought it would be good to up sticks and move to a different area; Solihull beckoned. The town had excellent links into Birmingham and it was the perfect place to raise a family; affluent and peaceful with excellent schools. We were living the suburban dream and loving it. My wage kept going up and as it did, so did our standard of living. The thing is, it never went up enough to create a gap between income and outgoings, but we kept getting things on credit, in anticipation of the next salary hike, so we never worried. There was never a safety cushion, but I wasn't too bothered about that. Nicer cars followed and we'd frequently go somewhere decent in the UK to have a holiday; not just your fortnight's break in the summer. Life was great and there were no concerns, so long as my salary kept coming in we'd be OK.

Looking back, I recognise how foolish it was to live like this, but I wanted to offer my family a certain lifestyle in spite of the credit risk.

Zoe kept going along to church throughout all the changes and although I wasn't interested in God, I'd still drive her and the kids along on a Sunday morning. In fact, even when Zoe was ill, I'd still take the kids. After all, they could believe in all the God stuff if they wanted, it just wasn't for me. When I'd drop them off, I'd wait in the car outside, doing some reading, listening to the radio, that kind of thing. I'd never set foot in the place though. That would have been ridiculous. After all, why did I need to believe in God when science gave me the answers I wanted and my life was pretty near perfect? Why did I need to rely on someone or something else? I had all the answers and I'd proved to the world that I could stand on my own two feet. As far as I could see, Christianity was there for you if you felt weak, but I was pretty strong.

When Zoe shared the news that she was pregnant with our third child, it really was the icing on the cake. I couldn't believe how great life was. It was as if everything had fallen into place and life was going to be one fantastic moment after the next. Zoe and I squabbled from time to time, but we had a solid marriage, two (nearly three) fantastic children and a great home

But then the letter arrived, and started something like a controlled panic. Slowly but surely, the pieces of my life flaked off one by one and stripped me of all my dignity. I had nowhere to hide and with Zoe expecting, there was even more pressure on our finances.

I couldn't apply for benefits once I'd worked my four weeks' notice, as I was technically self-employed and had my own Plc. I would have had to wind up the business and I didn't want to do that, so I had no choice but to resign myself to a desperate search for any kind of work to bring in some sort of income. The only thing I could find was some other small contract work, but it paid just one third of what I'd earned previously. It was a bitter pill to swallow; the pay difference was so massive and I felt ashamed. What's more, I knew in my heart of hearts that this was no long term solution. We simply couldn't meet the repayments and mortgage and we were slipping deeper and deeper into debt. I felt like my life was draining away down the plughole, an unstoppable slide into the abyss.

I tried to open up to Zoe about how I felt, but I didn't want her to be too alarmed about things, especially as her due date was getting closer and closer. I would try and keep things a secret, then the anxiety would hit home and I'd just blurt stuff out. She would often cry and then I'd get angry with her as a result 'Well if you have faith, why are you crying?' I'd say. Surely her God would get her through? I got more and more vocal about how Christianity wasn't true and how she'd been brainwashed into believing it. I spiralled into depression and I couldn't take the failure of not being able to provide financially for my family. I was so desperate to be a great father to my children and it broke my heart that I wasn't able to support the household on my income. It got to the stage where we were paying the mortgage but nothing else and then the harassment really picked up speed. Often the phone would ring, Zoe would pick it up and then there would be silence on the other end of the line; pure intimidation tactics from the people we owed money to.

Worse still was the stress Zoe was under in the latter stages of her pregnancy. I tried my best to shield it all from her, but she knew full well what was going on. It put such a strain on our relationship and I succumbed to going to the doctor as I was so depressed. I can remember walking into the surgery and wondering what on earth had happened to my life. I used to be so happy and had everything that I could want. Now I had been reduced to a fearful wreck, stumbling from one day to the next whilst trying desperately to keep a roof over my family's head. I just couldn't take it any more.

I walked into the GP's room, explained what was going on and just broke down. I sobbed and sobbed, thinking about all the things I'd lost and how inadequate I felt deep inside. The doctor was obviously concerned about me and prescribed me anti-depressants. I also paid a visit to the local Citizen's Advice Bureau and they recommended that I see a firm of solicitors nearby. When I went to my appointment with them, they suggested I go for an IVA, which was gut-wrenching. I spoke to Zoe about it and she suggested that I speak to Christians Against Poverty about our debt and see if they could offer an alternative route out. They had an office in the church Zoe went to in Solihull. The name put me off as I didn't want to accept help from people who believed in God, but I didn't have a choice, especially after Zoe showed me the literature to try to win me round. We simply had nowhere else to turn.

Throughout this traumatic process, Zoe seemed to be faring much better than me. She had her moments when she'd look worried and I even saw her cry a few times, but there was this peace about her that I secretly craved and was jealous of. In fact I would often get annoyed that it didn't seem to be affecting her as much as me. I'd goad her about it, wondering why she wasn't thinking about the bigger picture of our finances.

When Mike, the CAP Centre Manager came round, I was sceptical to say the least and I wasted no time in letting him know what I thought about God. 'I don't want the Christian stuff I just want help with the debt,' I said. It wasn't a great opener, but to my surprise, Mike wasn't offended and it certainly didn't alter his approach to our situation. He was non-judgemental and I loved that. There was no sense of being scolded for what we'd done. He never condoned our decision to base our whole lives on credit, but at the same time, he was prepared to work for us and with us to get a solution. I struggled at first in letting someone else deal with my debt, but by this stage my dignity was in tatters and I'd have accepted genuine help regardless of what I'd have to do. When Mike visited, Zoe had two weeks to go before giving birth. It was a traumatic time and I think Zoe focussed lots on the pregnancy to get her through. After all, it could have jeopardised the baby's health if she'd allowed herself to get really stressed about things.

Mike promised to come back with a budget that enabled us to pay back our debt but still eat properly and afford life's essentials. At the start of 2004, I had to make the ultimate sacrifice in my eyes at that time; in order to pay off the debts and draw a line under the situation, we had to sell the house. It was crushing; everything that I'd worked so hard to get, all that I'd tried to give to my family, obliterated in one go. At the time, I wasn't even happy that the debts had been paid off, instead, I was just devastated that the house had gone and we'd lost a beautiful family home. I felt like this was the ultimate failure for a husband and father and my depression got worse and worse.

The doctor put me on anti-depressants which helped to stop my mood swings, but they didn't stop me from feeling the pain; that was always present and nothing I could do would shift it. When our eldest son decided to get baptised at the age of seven, I desperately wanted to support him in spite of my opposition to Christianity. I think at the time I felt so conscious of how his world had been turned upside down that I wanted to show him I loved him at all costs and support him as a father. I felt I'd really let him down and I hoped that this would help to heal things between us. I hadn't set foot in a church in years and I braced myself for the baptism service. I think a year or so before, I would have refused to go into the church, but I was so broken by our situation that my defences went down and I agreed to go along.

The service went fine, but it still didn't change my mind about whether I believed in Jesus or not. I wasn't going to budge on that one, regardless of how upset I was. Zoe still seemed at peace about things though, which made me even more irritable. As the months went by, my depression got worse and worse. The drugs medicated me to a certain extent, but it didn't stop my behaviour from being awful sometimes. I think I hit rock-bottom at one of my son's birthday parties. I acted in a horrendous way. I was so angry and critical, lashing out at people for no good reason. It ruined the whole day. Afterwards, I felt ashamed and couldn't believe I'd been so horrible, especially as it was meant to be a special day for our children. It was at that point that I truly came to the end of myself.

In total desperation, I arranged an appointment to see one of the counsellors at Zoe's church and there was a waiting time of about two weeks. In the meantime, I was frantically looking for anything to support me and I went along to church with Zoe one Sunday morning. It was such a strange situation walking into the building that I had spent so much time waiting outside whilst my wife and kids went in each Sunday. A year before, if someone had suggested that I would set foot in the church I would have told them they were crazy. The thing is though, my guard was down and I wasn't in the mood for arguing for the sake of it. I knew I needed help and if it came from this church, then so be it. The Pastor, Dave, was doing a whole series on the different family roles seen from a Christian perspective and this particular Sunday was the turn for 'The Role of a Christian Father'.

It was like he was talking directly at me; each sentence tailor-made for where I was at. I was glued to the seat, unable to think about anything else. I felt challenged, encouraged, convicted, released all at the same time. When the service ended, I couldn't stop thinking about his words, I was so impacted by them. He was talking about the kind of father that I'd always wanted to be. The kind of father that I'd tried so hard to be but never quite managed to achieve. For the next two days, I couldn't stop thinking about Dave's words and it even stopped me from sleeping. Try as I might, I couldn't shake God off. Two days later I still wasn't sleeping and I threw down the gauntlet; 'Alright God, if you want me to believe, you're going to have to answer my questions.'

I still struggled with what I had learned about creation and geology at college; I couldn't reconcile what I read in the Bible with what I read from scientists, so I sided with the scientists and stopped believing in God. I logged on to the internet at about two in the morning and typed in 'Christian Geologists'. Instead of the search engine giving me a list of sites like normal, it just sent me direct to this website. I read and read and read and it was like God was answering all my questions directly through this site; all the things I'd disputed and thought couldn't be answered by the Bible were there in front of me; tailor-made answers from God to me. My heart pounded as I continued to read, I knew God was speaking to me. It was an incredible encounter with the creator of the universe and I was transfixed. I gave my life to God there and then, amazed by what God had done and so excited about the future, knowing that God loved me and was for me.

In my excitement, I ran upstairs and woke Zoe up; she was sound asleep but the excitement in my voice meant she came round quickly. 'I've just become a Christian' I said. 'God answered all my questions. I believe.' I think she was amazed by what had happened but was still half asleep. She hugged me and said, 'That's amazing,' and gave me a weak smile. 'Let's talk about it in the morning,' and then she turned over and went back to sleep. I wasn't sure if she had believed me when I told her then, but she certainly believed me when we talked the following morning. She was so amazing and supportive; little did I know how long she'd prayed to see that moment. My life had been well and truly turned around and I was full of hope about the relationship that God was waiting to have with me.

Zoe's story

Waiting for something for a long period of time can be hard. I prayed for Phil for ten years, desperately calling out to God that he would respond to his love and turn back to him. At times, I just felt like a voice calling out in the wilderness, wondering if God had heard me; wondering if my prayers would be answered soon or whether I'd have to wait until the end of Phil's life. God answered those prayers in the most incredible way and looking back, all that waiting was well worth it.

When Phil lost his job, I was upset with him because of the changes that I knew would have to take place in our lives, but throughout it all, I always had an abiding sense of God's peace and the fact that he was going to use it for our good. With our third son due around the time that things started to fall apart, it was a testing time for the whole family. Being a Christian doesn't make you immune to life's troubles, but it gives you a hope and a peace that recognises that God goes beyond our present circumstance and is there for us. Although there were times when I would cry about Phil losing his job and the resulting problems, I always knew God was there for us; I just wished that Phil would see that too.

At times, Phil would get angry and wonder why I was so peaceful when he was so traumatised. I didn't want to offer too much of an explanation as I felt deep down he knew it was because of my relationship with God. He would also glaze over when anyone started talking about God or worse; get angry and defensive. I found it desperately hard sometimes because I knew that if I started talking about God, that would be the end of our relationship. It was only in God's strength that I was able to maintain my poise. Throughout it all, I would pray that Phil would just come to the end of himself and turn to God and realise that he could find his strength in him. Watching someone you love so much go through real trauma and depression is such a hard thing. I thank God that he gave me the strength to keep crying out for Phil to come back to him and that he kept Phil from relying on his own strength.

When things got really bad with Phil's depression I did have moments when I wondered when it was all going to end; the phone would ring sometimes and then there would be silence on the other side of the line; proof that the creditors were trying to scare us. I struggled and I'd cry alone to stop Phil from seeing me and accusing me of having no faith.

After what seemed like an eternity, things started to turn around when our eldest son had a dream. He dreamt that he was crying out for his dad to come back to God. My son shared this with me and it filled me with hope as I knew that God was doing something in the whole of our family; mobilising our children to pray for their father too. Then, the following Sunday, the leader of the children's work at the church came up to me and told me that as they had prayed, God had told them that he was going to answer our son's prayer about Phil coming back to God and that I would just have to wait for it to happen. At the time, I was bowled over with how God had confirmed to me about Phil's relationship with him, but I was slightly daunted by the prospect of another ten years of praying!

God was so gracious to us though and moved a lot quicker than I had thought possible. Phil well and truly came to the end of his own strength through a series of events. As his depression worsened, his guard went down and he was more open to coming along to church; first to one of our son's baptism and second to a service where our pastor was preaching on the role of a Christian father. That service in particular really challenged him and he wasn't able to rest afterwards and found sleeping hard. A couple of nights later, he woke me up at about two o'clock in the morning to say that he had become a Christian, after God answered his questions directly through a website. I was amazed, stunned and shocked. I couldn't take it in at first, but I knew that he was sincere. I could just see the change in him, although I did roll over a few minutes later and go back to sleep!

The following morning was amazing, talking to Phil about how God had been on his case, wooing him back to him with real gentleness and patience. Through CAP, Phil had seen first hand how God's people could offer hope to him without being judgemental and I really believe that it helped to demolish some of the stereotypes that he had in his mind about Christians and God. It was a tough process, but so worth it. Life is still hard from time to time, but it is such a privilege to go through the challenges as a couple in faith that God is going to look after us and provide for us as a family. In my wildest dreams, I never would have imagined all the amazing things God has done for us. We are now truly a family going in the same direction, supported and held by God and his people; the Church. I love praying with Phil and sharing our hopes and dreams for the future. God has so much for us and we're only just starting to see that unfold.

If you are still crying out to God for a loved one to turn to him, never give up, because God never does. Those ten years were hard going, but God was working things out in his time; perfect time and the results are so beautiful that you look back and it's gone in the blink of an eye.

Janine, Andy and their three children

7. JUSTICE FULFILLED

Andy's Story

'What are you going to give up to build my church?'

The voice cuts clear across the auditorium. Immediately, I know this is a significant moment. One I will remember without the notes I have been writing so furiously. The future looks different. Dreams and hopes I had put to one side come alive again. God is asking me what I want to do. He wants me to take the first step. 'What do you want to do?' the speaker continues. It's as if God is giving me an invitation. Could it be that I have been waiting for God, when he has actually been waiting for me?

I'm in Chicago on what will be a life changing leadership conference. This is just the first session and we are being challenged on what it takes to be the leaders God wants for the Church. Now I feel that challenge directed specifically to me. There is something I can do. I don't have to wait to hear from God.

I've been working for CAP since April 2006, but looking back now I can see that a concern about poverty and injustice has been a part of my life from an early age. As I grew up, my parents would always impress on me and my two sisters how important it is to look out for those who are less privileged than us, to stand up for people and to have compassion for them.

My mum's family worked on the docks in Southampton. She would tell us stories of my grandfather arriving at the waterside in the morning, waiting to be told whether he had work for the day or not. The foreman would scatter tokens on the floor, each token representing work for the day. The men would then fight to get a token and a job. It must have been a very hard existence and that awareness of real working class poverty and grafting a living stayed with my mum. I can remember her saying how important the unions had been in those days, standing up for employees who had so few rights.

I saw my parents living out the values they wanted to teach us. It wasn't just that they had 'good morals', they really acted on them. We saw them giving to others in many different ways and that taught us generosity. It was ingrained in us as we were growing up that so many people had a lot less than we did and that we should be concerned about poverty and injustice.

As a teenager, a family friend at my parents' church got me involved with the charity, Tearfund. My awareness of poverty and injustice around the world increased and I learned how much God wanted the Church to be doing something about it. I did what many have done. I read books about the issues and what the Bible has to say. I gave donations and helped organise events. Even then, I wanted to do more, to be directly involved. There was a desire in me to stand up for people who weren't able to stand up for themselves and to fight against systems that were oppressing people. I didn't see why some of us should have so much when others were literally starving. At times I was frustrated as I didn't know what I could do to work this desire out in practice.

After leaving school, I studied law at university and became a solicitor. I married Janine, who I had met when we were both students and spent some time one summer working for a church in Tower Hamlets, East London. I joined a firm on the South Coast and over time began to specialise in employment law, representing clients at industrial tribunals. I also did some environmental work for a local company that ran quarries and landfill sites. It might not have seemed glamorous stuff, but I found it interesting and found myself wanting to do more. I started a course studying Environmental Law.

As a result, I eventually left the law firm and moved to a large building materials company that wanted an environmental lawyer for its quarrying and landfill business. I worked there for eleven years doing a whole range of things and being involved in some very interesting projects. The new job also saw us move up from the South Coast to Bracknell where we now live. It was a great time and at one point, there was the opportunity to move abroad and work in the Company's Legal Department in Germany. We moved out to Dusseldorf as a family and had a fantastic couple of years. It was a great experience for us and one which we will always look back on as a significant time in all our lives.

Even then, not everything worked out the way we thought it would. We had seen our time in Germany as an answer to prayers we had prayed as a church that people would be sent there with their jobs and help to build the Church in Germany. We had become part of a German speaking church and as we came to the end of our stay, we wondered whether God wanted us to stay on and be part of a church plant in the town where we were living. I applied for jobs which would have enabled us to stay but nothing came from any of the applications. After a while I felt God say very clearly that it was time to come home. I was reading a passage in the Bible where God tells Elijah, 'go back the way you came.' The words leapt out at me. I knew that there was something more, something just on the horizon, but I wasn't sure what it was. We moved back to Bracknell in expectation of what God would do next.

I grew up in a small, traditional Baptist church in London. People would joke with me about how long it would be before I stopped whatever I would be doing and headed for Bible College to train as a pastor. At the same time, there was a strong belief that you couldn't be a pastor or church leader until you had received 'the call' from God. Although I understand that belief, I think it really inhibited me from engaging with what God wanted me to do. I wasn't sure what it meant to hear this call. I was waiting for a clear, unequivocal sign from God and felt as if I couldn't start on anything until I'd had this sign. I often wondered if there was something else I should be doing, if I should be leaving my job to train to lead a church but I could never say that I had definitely heard God say that this is what he wanted for me. So I never took things any further. I would always come up against the question 'has God called you?' There was a time when I was very confused about what God wanted from me but felt him say that working in a secular job was just as much full time service as working in a church. That carried me through my work as a solicitor. I knew that God wanted me to have an impact for him wherever I was working.

But the thought that there was something else for me was always there and, of course, my understanding was changed in an instant on that visit to America. It was one of those moments when God just changes your thinking on something completely and, in a moment, everything becomes clear. That moment really did change the direction of my life and led me to where I am now.

The conference I was on was the annual leadership summit at Willow Creek. It was a real privilege to be there as part of a team with the senior pastor of our church. This was the first session of the conference and Bill Hybels was talking on 'Passing the Leadership Test'. It was just one section of the final part of his talk that changed my life forever.

'Some people get a very specific call from God to do something in the church', he said. 'They might get asked to do something specific at a particular time in a particular place.' He likened this to being conscripted. 'For the majority of us, however, God paints a vision of what the Church can be. He then asks simply, "What are you going to give up to build that church? What are you going to leave behind? What can you offer?"'

And that was it. That was the moment when everything changed. I realised that I had a choice and could start doing things for God, without needing to have that audible 'call'. I returned to the UK with a new-found passion and excitement.

At that time, Janine and I were heading up small groups in our church in Bracknell. I approached my boss at work and asked if I could go part time to work on this. He very kindly agreed to let me have a day off a week. Slightly more worryingly, he also asked whether one day was enough to achieve what we wanted to achieve and did I need more! Perhaps they wanted me out of the office!

Leading small groups was another great experience for us. We had a great team of leaders around us and we had the chance to work out ideas we had and put them into practice. We saw the potential of small groups to change lives. We wanted to see small groups of people expressing their love for each other in such a way that anyone looking in would see that God was there. We borrowed a phrase from Willow Creek; we wanted to build communities that would change the community.

That was 2003 and 2004. As we came to the end of 2004, we had some very difficult news. Janine had been suffering with pain in her hip and pelvis for a long time and was finding it difficult to walk. She had seen various doctors but we had never got to the root of the problem. In December 2004, we finally saw an Orthopaedic Consultant who confirmed that Janine had a rare form of bone cancer.

The next year was obviously very difficult for us as a family. We knew that sometimes God allows things to happen in our lives that we don't understand but now we were experiencing that first hand.

At times, it was very difficult to see that God was involved at all. There were times when Janine felt she had been abandoned. Now we can look back and see just how much God was involved. We know that our relationships with him have deepened considerably and that our perspective of what matters to him has been changed profoundly.

We had incredible support from family and friends and particularly our church. So much was done for us as Janine was in and out of hospital for what seemed like forever. My company were amazing to me and let me have what was effectively nine months compassionate leave so that I could be with Janine. I remember that I went into the office one day and my boss just said, 'What are you doing here? Get up to the hospital and be with your wife!' Our kids were also amazing during this time. It must have been traumatic for them but they have come through it so well. We are very proud of them.

Eventually, the treatment came to an end and Janine recovered. Despite intensive chemotherapy, however, the tumour could only be removed by amputating her left leg. For the last three years we have been learning to live with a disability that Janine never expected to have – though she still tries to live life at 110mph and is a great Support Worker for me!

Whilst Janine was ill, the company I was working for was bought out by another company and voluntary redundancy was offered to all of us. I was given a chance to stay but I knew that this was the moment I had been waiting for to make a change. In a step of faith, I decided to take the redundancy though not sure what God was going to do next.

I see now that God had been leading, directing and providing for us to get us where we are now. I had heard that the church was hoping to set up a debt counselling centre in partnership with CAP and thought it sounded really interesting. When Simon, who is now our Senior Pastor, approached me and said the Elders thought it might be me who should be the Centre Manager, I dived into 'Nevertheless' (the book which tells the story of CAP) and read all I could. It wasn't long before I thought, 'Yes, I think this is me'.

The desire I had for standing up for the poor and needy and representing those without a voice had never left me and now I realised that working for CAP would tap straight into those desires.

I would be able to tackle poverty in the local community, using the skills I'd learnt as a lawyer and at the same time be able to tell people about God's love for them. All those years previously when I was studying Law, I had never realised that God would be able to use those skills to enable me to stand up for some of the most marginalised and destitute people in our society. It's a long way from running planning inquiries for quarries with a commercial firm, but God has taken us step by step. I look back to the church we were a part of on the South Coast. It was in the middle of a very deprived area and I can see now that the experience we had there and the things we learnt from our pastor are all part of the experience I needed for my role with CAP. Even whilst at University, I remember being impressed by one of the tutors who had given up a highly paid career in the city to study and practice Social Welfare Law. I thought that sounded like something I would want to do and here was the chance. Towards the end of my time as a lawyer, we were involved in the sale of a business where we worked forty-eight hours without sleep just to get the deal completed. It was not as glamorous as people would make out and I remember thinking 'If I am going to be working this hard then I don't want it to be just to make money for people who are already rich, I want it to count for something'.

What I do with CAP, speaking up for people and bringing them hope and a solution really excites me and is very rewarding. It is hard work and it comes at a price but it is a price that we are willing to pay. Some of the situations we come across are desperate and the needs are overwhelming. A verse from the Bible that has always been a challenge to me is Isaiah 58:10 where we are told to 'spend' ourselves on behalf of the hungry. I love what that verse says about needing to give ourselves to helping the poor. Early on in my time as a Centre Manager, a friend told me that whenever he saw me and thought of CAP, the word 'relentless' came into his mind. I am sure this was in the positive sense of the word and I know God wants me to be relentless in helping people and pursuing justice in all the situations we come across. I have that word stuck to the wall above my computer as a reminder. I also know that I need to keep the balance and resist doing more than I should be doing, leaving room for God to work.

There is certainly an impact on family life. My children joke with me about having given up being a lawyer to be a 'charity worker' and denying them the lifestyle they think they might have had. I tell them that, although it's true we have less money, I would never have wanted us to have that lifestyle anyway. They also see the impact in terms of time and energy. They say that I am obsessed with what I do and are quick to remind me of where their CAP responsibility ends! Underneath, I know how much they admire CAP and support what we are doing. I love the fact that they are growing up seeing first hand what it means for Christians and churches to be serving the poor. I want them to carry that into their own experience and choices in life. I also know that I could not be doing what I am doing without the support of the whole family and their willingness to be involved.

Some people would think that the sacrifices we've made are above and beyond what we should have, but the truth is that we're not doing this alone. We are supported by a fantastic extended family – our church. Again, the truth is we wouldn't be able to do this work without being part of it. Our church is a great environment in which to run a CAP Centre.

Simon, our senior pastor, has always been one hundred per cent behind me and the work we do. In fact, the whole church is supportive. I might be the one going into people's homes and helping them at the point of crisis, but we need a body of people who will love clients as they become part of the church community. I would not be able to do this work without the church. I also have an excellent team of Support Workers who come out with me. I can help clients to some extent, but I can't provide the support network they need. That's where the church comes in.

And of course, it isn't all 'one way traffic'. Through CAP we are reaching people we would not otherwise have reached. Through the steady steam of clients who have become part of the church, we are becoming far more representative of the community around us and a more diverse body of people. Whilst we might have changed people through CAP, they have also changed us. The church is literally being transformed through CAP clients.

We recently moved over to a new model of running our centre that will enable us to see far more clients each year. We want to expand further and our vision is to have a centre that will be able to see at least two-hundred clients a year. Currently, we can only see about half that amount. We want to get to the position where we are not just scratching the surface but having a discernible impact on the levels of debt and poverty across Bracknell and the surrounding area. I can't wait to see all those extra lives turned around by God's love and the service we offer. It's going to be a very exciting time for us and I know that the church is ready for the challenge.

Speaking personally, I've been changed by the work too. I like to feel I am in control in life but I'm having to learn a far greater dependence on God. I know I am involved in something that matters vitally to him and in which nothing will happen without him. There is nothing like working in this area for learning just how urgent our praying needs to be.

Since starting to work for CAP there is definitely a heightened sense of adventure in my life. In what other job would you be invited into someone's home to help them when they're in crisis? It still amazes me that I get to pray with people who are often far from God. I remember walking back to the station after my interview in Bradford and wondering whether we would be the first centre in CAP history never to see anyone saved and whether I was really gifted for the job. I sensed God tell me 'just do the work of an evangelist and leave the rest to me'. It has been amazing to see people respond to Jesus, find faith in him and become part of the church.

It is simply the greatest privilege to be able to offer people hope when they think there is none. I still love taking paperwork away from clients and seeing the relief on their faces as they realise there is now someone working and standing with them. Before I started with CAP, I'm not sure I realised the poverty I would see in what is supposed to be the prosperous South East. To see people who have gone hungry as they try to meet debt repayments still affects me deeply. It's a great moment handing over a financial statement to a client and then explaining that they can start spending more on food because we have prioritised their debts and negotiated repayments with their creditors.

Another rewarding moment for me is going to court with a family threatened with an eviction and having that eviction suspended. It feels good to be back in my old environment but this time using the court to keep someone in their home – and then not have to charge them for the advice. For the client, the fear before the hearing can be almost unbearable. There is incredible relief when they come out knowing that they have been given another chance. We head for coffee and it has never tasted so good. Last year alone we saved hundred of families from eviction throughout the charity. That's what gets me really excited; seeing justice done for the poor, needy and most overlooked people in society.

The most important aspect of the job will always be the lives that are transformed. I think about a whole number of clients who were on the verge of suicide because of their debt and who are now free to enjoy life again. I also think about Bob and Karen*. When Bob first called us to tell us about the debt they were in, he was desperate and didn't think anyone could help them. I remember going round to their house for the first visit with the incredible sense that God was going to do something. They say that it was as if a friend had arrived. I remember thinking that I had arrived at friends. In time, Bob and Karen came to Alpha events and then they both started attending church on a Sunday morning. One morning in January, they responded to an appeal to become Christians, along with two other clients. That was an amazing moment. Since then they have been baptised and are now a much loved part of the Church. Their story has been an

---

*Name changed to protect identity

inspiration to others and they have both been out with me to see new clients. To me it just doesn't get any better then seeing lives turned around like that. It is what being the church is all about.

I have never felt so strongly that I am in the right place at the right time, doing what I am meant to be doing. I am so grateful that working for CAP and the Church has given me that opportunity. I can honestly say that the last two years of my life have been the best so far.

8. FREEDOM

Julia's Story

The alarm goes off. It's seven o'clock. I take a deep breath and prepare to put my 'happy face' on for the twins. I get up, get dressed and go downstairs. Almost robotically, I say 'morning' to Felicity and Adam, check they're OK, make their lunch and get them ready. A few minutes later we're in the car driving to school.

Returning home, I look around the house. There's a pile of washing that needs sorting, the carpets need vacuuming and there are dirty plates in the sink. 'I'll do those later,' I think, and crawl back into bed. I snuggle into my duvet, hiding from the world, and escape to the paradise of sleep.

I am brought back into life with a jolt. The phone is ringing. My heart starts beating faster and faster, my hands turn sweaty and my breathing quickens. I pull the duvet over my head and try to block out the sound.

Shaking, I hear a knock on the door. Slowly I creep to the window and try to see who it is. There's a strange man standing at my door. I don't know who he is, but I suspect he is a debt collector coming to challenge me about my debts. He glances around and I quickly duck out of view. I crawl on the floor and hide back in my bed. The panic attack is getting worse, I can hardly breathe, but am paralysed with fear. How long can I go on like this? Tears fall down my cheeks and I feel like a prisoner in my own home. Maybe I should rid myself of all of this fear and commit suicide? But then what about the twins? I can't bear to have them return to my ex-husband. No, I must stay alive for them. But oh how I wish this would end.

After what seems like hours, I pluck up the courage to walk downstairs. All is quiet and I think it's safe to move around. My stomach's rumbling anyway and I need some food. I walk down the stairs and see a pile of post on the floor. I daren't look at it, I can't face what might be in those letters. After all, one letter told me I would go to prison. I don't need that kind of stress right now. Gingerly I pick up the letters and put them in a pile with all the others. When I feel strong again I will take a look, but not now.

Going into the kitchen I reach into the cupboard and take out bags of crisps and chocolate. It's all I can stomach right now, plus it's a comfort to eat them. Not so good for my waist line. My trousers are getting tighter and I know I'm piling on the pounds. But I just can't eat anything else.

I think back to life in Tamworth when I had lost two stone, went to the gym five times a week and had been part of 'Weight Watchers'. Here I am now, fourteen stone and feeling disgusting. I've lost all respect for myself.

I look at the clock. Just half an hour and I can pick up the kids. Not enough time to do the washing then. How I long for them to come home and distract me from this nightmare. Somehow being around them brings a calmness to me. I revert back to automatic pilot as I leave the house, looking around first to make sure no-one is going to see me get into the car. I've made it through another day.

Just a few months ago this was what life was like for me. It all started when I divorced my husband in January 2005 and moved to Hemel Hempstead.

I met Mike* in the early 1990s. We were working at the same office in Tamworth. Both of us had been married before and I suppose we were looking for people different to our former partners. In September 1995, I bought a house and Mike moved in with me. A year later I

*Name changed to protect identity

gave birth to twins, Felicity and Adam, and I married Mike the following July.

At the time I knew it wasn't right, but thought Mike was a decent person and surely everything would be OK. We had the twins, and I wanted it to work out. I suppose I was in denial about the whole relationship.

Soon after the twins were born, I realised that I would need to go back to work. Initially I worked as a part-time temp at Boots. I loved it, but it didn't bring in enough. So I went to work for a housing developer. However, all my salary just went on childcare.

During this time I knew my marriage wasn't healthy. Mike just couldn't communicate. He would never talk to me and treated me just like a lover and nothing else. We weren't even friends. I became ill with depression, but just dealt with it by working longer hours.

I became more depressed, and my husband became increasingly distant. I started taking Felicity to Sunday School. I was searching for something to help ease the internal strain caused by my marital problems.

Life went on like this for two years and then we got to crunch point. Mike was into pornography, which I found disgusting. I hated it. One day my son Adam was just playing on the computer and went to click on the 'My Music' folder. Thankfully I was watching him because Mike had stored a whole load of pornographic images and videos in that file. I couldn't believe it. Didn't he know that our children could accidentally access those files?

It really was the last straw. I went to see a solicitor and started divorce proceedings immediately. As soon as my husband found out, life became intolerable at home. The atmosphere was one of anger and mental abuse. Mike no longer spoke to me but just shouted all the time. I was terrified, but more frightened for the kids. He never hit me, but came close to it on a number of occasions. I knew I had to get out of the house and protect my children.

I wasn't sure what to do. I couldn't stay in the house, but knew that living on my own would be difficult as I could only work part-time with the twins.

In the end, I decided to move to Hemel Hempstead in Hertfordshire as my family live in that area. So I sold the house, but only got £30,000 from the sale. I found a three-bedroom cottage, paid the first six months rent and got a part-time job in an estate agents in St. Albans. Although things were tight, everything was OK. I had debts from my marriage (all the debts were in my name), but was able to keep on top of the payments.

Problems started shortly after I started work. My boss was a bully. He had serious anger-management problems to such an extent that he would throw phones and computers across the office when in a rage. It wasn't just me he picked on, but all the staff. He would shout, rant and rave at us on a daily basis. I managed to stand up for myself occasionally, but hated what he was doing to the staff. In the end I raised a grievance procedure against him but the stress of it was too much and I had a mini-breakdown. Despite my grievance, the company did nothing about this man, so it was impossible to return to work even when I started to feel better.

Being off sick was a disaster for my financial situation. Because I was only on statutory sick pay I started to get behind with my rent and debt repayments. It was then that the phone calls and letters began. My mental health deteriorated too, and I simply could not handle the pressure. All I could do was function enough to look after the children.

On a good day I would try to phone the creditors and explain my plight and ask to pay the minimum repayment, but they just shouted abuse at me and wouldn't listen. By the end of the phone call, I was more upset then when I started. I received threatening letters telling me that I would even end up in prison – I was terrified. I started having panic attacks, and would hardly leave the house except to take the kids to school. My life simply consisted of taking the twins to school and sleeping.

Eventually my landlord gave me a notice to move out because I wasn't paying the rent. He took me to court and got us evicted from the house. On 6 November 2007, we were evicted and the Council put us into temporary accommodation; a one-bedroom flat.

The Council decided that I had purposefully made us homeless by not paying the rent. They thought that I had enough money to pay the rent and just hadn't. They didn't seem to take my breakdown into consideration. It was so unjust.

The flat they put us into was disgusting. Unfortunately, I wasn't able to see the flat before my son Adam saw it. He had been sent home from school due to a headache, most likely the result of the stress and anxiety of the move. The flat was in this huge house. As I climbed the stairs, my heart was breaking. It was so dirty and certainly didn't feel safe enough for two children. When I entered the flat I just gasped. It was revolting. Mess everywhere, all the surfaces were filthy, it smelt horrible. There was no way I wanted to bring my precious children into such an environment.

Luckily a friend offered to house us while I cleaned up the flat. In my original home I lived next to two wonderful people, Denise and Tim. They were both Christians and really supportive of me. Denise helped me sort out the flat. Everyday for a week we scrubbed, disinfected and cleaned the entire place. We worked so hard in that week.

So I moved in with the twins on the Sunday. Although the flat was now clean, Adam and Felicity were very distressed. They were scared of the place and upset by how small the flat was. I tried to put on a brave front, and just told them to pretend it was an adventure.

Against the odds, I managed to turn the flat into a home. Once I shut the door I felt safe, but the rest of the house was riddled with drug takers and I certainly didn't want my children to get sucked into that.

I had heard about Christians Against Poverty a few months before we moved into the flat, as a friend was working with them. However, I was in such a muddle that I couldn't make the call. I was so afraid that I would be judged, and to be honest, I didn't want to admit that I had problems. But when faced with living in a one-bed flat in a house full of drug users, reality certainly hit home.

I made the call to Owen Cooper, Centre Manager for CAP's Hemel Hempstead centre, at the end of November. On 2 December he came to visit.

I remember my first impression of Owen. He was so kind, warm, friendly and extremely caring. Most importantly though, he never judged me. He arrived with his wife, Kerry-Ann, who said she was a Support Worker for me. I'm a sociable person and so warmed to them immediately. Owen looked at the pile of letters and said, 'Just give them to me, you don't need to worry any more.' All I need to do now is focus on one payment a month and everything is done for me. It is so wonderful to be released from all the complications of debt.

Throughout that visit, I just cried and cried. It was such a relief. It was like a whole weight was lifted off me. Owen then offered to pray for me. I had been a Christian, had been confirmed in my thirties and was a regular church-goer, but had fallen away from that life. Yet there was something different about Owen and Kerry-Ann. There was a peace and tranquillity that came in with them and that feeling of warmth came around me – it was lovely!

Owen asked me if I wanted to recommit to God. I said 'yes please' and completely broke down. At that moment God came back into my life again. From that first visit I felt very secure and knew I would be guided in the right way.

Kerry-Ann started to call me every week and take me out for coffee and cake. We have now become really great friends. Owen also came back with a financial statement and a budget for me. Now all I do is pay a certain amount into my CAP Account, CAP then distribute this to pay all my bills and debts, and I have enough left over for food and other expenses.

I find going to church difficult because of my emotional difficulties, but did go on an Alpha course a few months ago at a church in Chorley Wood with Denise. It's a big church, but I met some lovely people. It was really helpful to find out more about God.

The best moment was when I went on the church Alpha Away Day. I was a bit nervous because I had heard about people falling on the floor when people prayed for them and I certainly didn't want anything like that to happen to me! However, I had the most amazing experience. I managed to wipe all the thoughts from my head. Tears were pouring down my face, but I had no thoughts in my head, just a sense of peace. It felt like the sun was shining on my face – I felt so warm, it was just the most lovely experience. Since that day, I have been changing gradually. I still have problems, but feel much calmer about them and am able to give more of my thoughts to God.

While all this was happening, my home situation was becoming worse. Because the Council had only put us into temporary accommodation they needed us to leave, but we didn't have anywhere else to go. They still believed that I had intentionally made myself and my children homeless.

I decided to fight against this judgement. I found a solicitor in London who would act on my behalf on legal aid. However, even though the council were sent medical reports regarding my mental health, I lost the appeal and then couldn't afford to pay the legal costs to continue with it.

It was so frustrating. There is no way that I would purposefully have made me and my twins homeless. I couldn't believe that the Council weren't taking my medical history into account. It seemed so unfair and I wasn't going to just sit back and take it. I felt that the Council was wrong and I needed more help.

I didn't want anyone else to suffer in the way I was, so I went to the press. They reported on my story and as a result the Council offered me a rent guarantee scheme. This meant that if I could find the first month's rent and deposit they would rent a property to me. Some good news at last.

We were removed from our flat at the end of January 2008. But despite being part of that scheme I didn't have anywhere to go, so we moved in with friends. I'd only been staying with my friend for three days when I received a phone call from Owen.

He said he'd just had a call from a Christian man who had read of my plight in the newspaper. This man (who wanted to remain anonymous) was offering me his home to rent at whatever price I could afford! I was completely speechless. I couldn't believe this man would be willing to offer me a home, especially when he didn't even know me.

He even offered to pay the council tax and TV licence! He said that we could stay there for as long as we wanted.

As if this wasn't enough, when I saw the house my jaw dropped even further. It was a beautiful four-bedroom detached house with a study, huge lounge, a dining room and even a garden. I just cried when I saw it – I was so amazed by this man's generosity.

I got the keys on 1 April 2008, and once all the electrics had been sorted we moved in on 19 April. I've been here five months now and I absolutely love it.

CAP advised me that because my debts were so big, that bankruptcy was my best solution. So on 16 July I went bankrupt and am now debt-free! I was scared at first and was worried about the humiliation of going bankrupt, but received so much support. I found out that going bankrupt was not really something to worry about. So I'm debt-free and living in a beautiful house. I am keeping to my budget, and paying regularly into my CAP Account – it's great. It's a completely fresh start for me and my family.

I have re-joined 'Weight Watchers' and am losing weight; I've lost nineteen pounds so far. I go to my local church every Wednesday for Communion – it's very traditional, but really helps me feel close to God.

My relationship with the twins is also getting better. The stress of the debt was taking its toll and I would shout at them a lot. But now I am so much calmer and we have fewer arguments. We have been brought closer together through this whole experience. They are even going to the 'Accelerate' course at Owen's church. This course looks at the wider problems in the world from a Christian perspective. They love the course and it's great to see them drawing closer to God. I love them so much and am really proud of the way they have come through this so strongly.

I also don't worry as much as I used to. My stress and depression is a lot better. I am working with the Community Health team and have seen a psychiatrist, who has given me new anti-depressants, which seem to be helping.

I have also become a Support Worker for Owen. I just love the fact that I can pass on my experience to someone else. I don't want anyone to feel like I felt. Debt is such a lonely and dark place to be in. If I can help bring light into those dark situations, then that makes it all worthwhile.

Owen and Kerry-Ann have asked me to share my story at church one Sunday. At one time I would have felt too humiliated to tell anyone, but not any more. I am excited. I have the love of God around me so I have nothing to feel ashamed about.

As a result of CAP and God's help I'm being healed from the past. Living in this great house is so wonderful and an amazing place to recover and rebuild my brokenness. I am even looking for a new job and had an interview just last week. I am so much more positive about life and a lot happier. We have a roof over our heads, I am getting better and I have God in my life – what else do you need?

I am so grateful to CAP. They provided a light at the end of the tunnel for me. I still work with them to pay all my bills and know I can rely on them for everything. CAP is my safety net, but most importantly, they are the living extension of Jesus to me.

Nigel & Emily.

9. FAITH

Emily & Nigel's Story

I'm crouching in the corner of my living room. I daren't move; I feel paralysed with fear. I've put a towel over the TV to block out the sound, but I hear these strange voices in my head and I don't know what to do. I feel like everyone is out to get me. They are talking about me all the time – I can't make it stop.

We need some food and Nigel wants me to go out to the supermarket, but I can't go. Last time I went out I struggled through twenty panic attacks just going round the shop. The thought of even going to the corner shop fills me with terror – I'll have to send the kids.

My medication is so powerful that I feel like a zombie. It is just so awful. I know that Nigel is suffering too. He has depression and I feel so guilty that I am adding more burdens to his life. I simply can't go on like this. I want it all to go away. I love my family, but I just don't want to live any more.

That was me, Emily, just a few months ago. But then we discovered CAP and our lives changed forever.

I married Nigel in 1986 when we were sixteen and seventeen, and have three beautiful children, Gareth (seventeen), Bethany (fifteen) and Melissa (thirteen). I love them; absolutely love them! They are the most amazing children. Gareth is one in a million, Bethany has such a pure heart and just wants to help people. She has a hard front, but a soft centre. Melissa, well she's my baby! She is so great. We have four gorgeous dogs and live in Leeds. We moved to Leeds six years ago after growing up in Middlesbrough. I don't work, but Nigel works in a tile warehouse. He is such a great man. So faithful and so loving – he is a rock to me and my family.

Our lives were almost pulled apart when we found ourselves in financial crisis. People get into debt for all sorts of reasons; it doesn't matter how you get there, you just need to do something about it. Me and Nigel weren't extravagant in our spending, but it's hard to say no to the kids. I love my children and wanted to buy them nice things – as any parent does. You think you can just pay for things later but it builds up. It's only when life changes that you realise things are getting out of control, and that's how it was with us.

The threatening calls, the letters and the banging on the door did little to ease my fragile mental state. I was so scared that I would send the kids to the front door to tell the bailiffs I wasn't in whilst I hid upstairs. Can you imagine how painful it is as a parent to be sending your kids to face these men? I felt so ashamed, but physically I couldn't do anything else. However, if I was feeling angry I would confront them myself. The anger would overcome any fears and I would shout at them, telling them in no uncertain terms to go. They couldn't take anything anyway as we had nothing to give.

With letters arriving from creditors telling me they were going to take us to court and other such threats I was always on edge. The constant worrying was just so tiresome. Trying to find ways to sort out the state we were in took its toll on our marriage. It didn't help that I thought Nigel was just ignoring it all, burying his head in the sand. It caused so many arguments and fights. It was simply getting too much to bear. I just didn't know what to do, we felt like such failures as parents. It's awful not being able to buy your kids the stuff they want, especially when they keep asking you.

My cousin, Hannah,* lives in Middlesbrough and she had been in a similar situation. She told me about this organisation called Christians Against Poverty and how they'd helped her. Julie Parker,

*Name changed to protect identity

the Centre Manager for CAP in Teesside, had really provided Hannah with an amazing solution.

After talking to my cousin and hearing all about CAP I decided to take the plunge and pick up the phone. Dialling that number was so scary. I was absolutely terrified. I thought I'd be judged and told off. I thought they'd look down their nose at me.

I dialled the number and a lady called Pam picked up the phone. The first thing I thought was how kind she sounded and I thought that she might just be alright. We talked for ages and really hit it off. Pam put me so much at ease and even offered to pray for me. I'd always thought I knew God because I did pray, but I was simply getting on with life. Me and Nigel had gone to a Billy Graham event aged seventeen and had stood up to respond. But I hadn't felt any different and we'd just got on with our lives. However, I did always try and teach my children to love God.

I remember my first meeting with Pam. I remember thinking 'she's posh!' Little did I know! On that first meeting we had such a laugh. Pam had got hopelessly lost and had ended up parking in the local sex shop car park! I thought, 'Well, if she's willing to park there, she can't be too posh!'

During that visit, Pam went through our finances with us. It felt like such a burden was being lifted. Me and Nigel are terrible with budgeting, so to have CAP come and do it all for us was amazing. After the meeting, Pam offered to pray for us. Nigel was an atheist and didn't believe in God, but I just said I wanted peace. My life had been so consumed with worry, paranoia and depression – I just wanted to be released. I needed peace.

Unbeknown to Pam, my youngest daughter Melissa had been listening whilst eating her breakfast. Just before we prayed she jumped up and said, 'I believe in God and I've been looking for him.' She'd been catching a minibus to a church in Bramley. Pam asked us if she could explain God to Melissa, so we said yes. There and then, Melissa decided to become a Christian. I didn't know what to think. But when Pam prayed for me, I did begin to feel at peace. After Pam's visit, for the first time in ages, both me and Nigel slept through the night! It was bliss!

A few days later, someone knocked on the door. It was a lady wearing crazy clothes with bright pink hair. Pam alleges that she had told me about this visit, but I'm not convinced! She said her name was Julie and that she lived just up the road and was a Support Worker for Pam. She asked if she could come in for a cup of tea, but stayed two hours! My son Gareth was like, 'Who is this woman and why is she in our house?' Little did he know!

She had brought a teen Bible for Melissa and invited her to a cell group at her house on Friday. Melissa said she'd only go if I went too! That was the last thing I wanted to do. I still found it hard to get out of the house and certainly didn't want to go without Nigel.

However, Mel is very persuasive and as I was beginning to feel more at peace within myself and stronger as a person I thought, 'Why not give it a chance?' So we went round to Julie's, only to discover that everyone was meeting at the pastor's house! A guy from Cambodia was apparently talking about something. So off we went to Pastor Ian's. I enjoyed the night and found people really friendly, but it was still early days and I wasn't about to jump into something I wasn't ready for.

When Pam had visited us, she'd left a copy of her testimony for me to read. I didn't read it whilst she was with us, but did after she'd left. Wow, her testimony was amazing! I thought if God could do that for her, he might be able to help me. When I asked Pam, she told me that Jesus could help me and do the same for me as he had for her. So I said I'd think about it. Pam invited me to a client event on the Saturday and then to a special women's group in the evening. I said I would come, but still wasn't ready to make that final decision.

I went to the events and had a great time. I just couldn't get over how friendly people were. I didn't really have any friends, but these people welcomed me as I was! I used to think that people disliked me and would never accept me. But meeting church people made me feel different. I didn't feel like these people were after me. It was such a relief!

That night something just felt right. I was alone in my bedroom and just wanted out. I didn't want to feel like I was failing any more – I just wanted to feel God's love. I asked him to show me his love and I felt it! It was like electricity running through my body – it was amazing! After that I slept so well.

The next day I went to Pam's church. Once a month they worship at the City Varieties Club in Leeds. The worship was incredible! I just felt so close to God. Pastor Ian then asked if anyone would like to be adopted by God. He invited people forward, so I went along with Melissa and my son Gareth. When I went forward on that Sunday, I felt the love of God again. I just felt so close to him and felt like I had no pain and no worries.

Gareth had also gone to some youth cell events with Melissa. I could see that he was changing, he was becoming so much more confident about himself and who he was. It was incredible that he came to church with us and then went forward to become a Christian. What a day!

Becoming a Christian completely healed my depression! It has given me a whole new outlook on life and I feel like a new person! I want to go out now and enjoy being around people once more.

My whole family has noticed the change in me. Nigel came home from work one day and said 'Where's your Ma?' to the kids. Normally I would be in because of my paranoia and fear, but I'd gone out just because I could! Melissa is just amazed by the radical transformation she's seen in me. She says, 'You always used to be in, but now you're always out!' I'm no longer paranoid either. I just don't care whether people are talking about me or not.

I also pray with more fervency and I love reading the Bible! My favourite verse is Jeremiah 29:11.

"'For I know the plans I have for you," declares the LORD, "Plans to prosper you and not to harm you, plans to give you hope and a future". It reminds me that God doesn't want to harm me. He has a plan for me! For my future! He is giving me hope and will prosper me. I don't mean with lots of money, but spiritually. For someone who has been as depressed and suicidal as I have, I can't tell you how much it means to know this amazing God of hope.

My story doesn't end there. My daughter Bethany still didn't know God and neither did Nigel. I so desperately wanted them to experience God's love like me, Melissa and Gareth had.

Bethany started coming to church with us and to the youth cells with the other two. Again, Bethany just got to a point where it felt right. She decided to become a Christian too! Bethany is now so much calmer, and no longer gets into trouble at school. She's blossoming into an amazing daughter.

That left just one, my wonderful husband Nigel. He is the love of my life and has been so amazing throughout everything that I've been through. Nigel is a great dad and an amazing husband. I call him 'My Bagpuss!' I love him so much.

Nigel used to go to Sunday School as a child and had gone to the Billy Graham event with me in the 1980s, but said he no longer believed. The church he used to go to had just preached at him – it had put him right off. However, Gareth invited him to church. He said, 'Come on Dad, you'll like it – it's really modern'. It was difficult to find a time for Nigel to come because he works most Sundays, but eventually a date was found.

When Nigel came to church I could tell he was moved. When Pastor Ian asked if anyone wanted to know God personally, Nigel was shaking. It was like he was stopping himself from getting up! I decided to go outside, because I knew he wouldn't get up if I was there! So I left and Julie, our cell leader, came up to Nigel and asked him why he wouldn't get up. Nigel said he wanted to. Gareth came over and led Nigel to Christ! I just couldn't believe it. My son was sitting there with my husband, leading him to salvation. I couldn't believe my family could be impacted in such a way.

Nigel says that it was the change in me that was the tipping point for him.

Nigel is changing too. He's stopped swearing and is healing from his depression. He has such a servant heart and, as Pam says, is just a really caring teddy bear. He looks out for others and is so kind.

As a family and as a couple, we are transformed. Nigel and I laugh so much more – we laugh like we used to and aren't worried. We certainly don't worry about the debt! We just send everything to CAP and they sort it out. We know what we need to pay and when to pay it – Pam says we are 'model clients!' Who'd have thought it two months ago?

I am also much calmer. I talk to my children rather than shout and even handle confrontation much better. For example, someone came round to my house to complain about Bethany. I wanted to smash her face in, but instead spoke calmly to this woman and even prayed for her when I returned to my house. This would never have happened four months ago!

I'm seeing changes in my children too. They are typical teenagers, but they are arguing less and are so polite and considerate. They are all just so much happier, which as a parent is great to see. They are getting involved in church and I just love it. Bethany and Melissa have even started 'treasure hunting' with the church.

Treasure hunting involves a group from the church meeting at the market or a local shopping centre and asking God to highlight people to us who he wants us to talk to. It's very scary, but really great! Once God has put a picture into your head like someone with a pain in their leg, or someone in a red coat, you look out for that person. When you see them, you go and ask if you can pray for them. Some people say yes, others no – but people are always moved and seeds are planted. When Bethany and Melissa took part, they felt God telling them to pray for a lady with a pink pram. They found that lady and she did want prayer! Amazing! I was so proud of them doing this.

I didn't think life could get any better, but then on 1 June, my entire family got baptised! What an amazing day. Julie and Chris from the cell group baptised Nigel. Then Nigel and Julie baptised me, and then me and Nigel baptised our three children. It was just fantastic! Pam was crying and I could hardly speak. Nigel was so proud to be involved in baptising the four of us. I loved baptising my children. It was the icing on the cake! Pam is so proud of us too. We're such good friends and I can't thank her enough for coming into my family in our hour of need.

We are all now involved in church. I love it! I go to cell group on a Wednesday and Friday, and we have such a laugh. God's so much fun – he's never boring. I love that my cell group doesn't take it all too seriously. I feel free to laugh like I haven't laughed in ages. Pam can't believe that I'm the same woman. We have lots of friends, we go and visit them, and they come round. I could never have imagined this.

Our finances are getting sorted and we will be debt free in less than three years! We now have money to live. It's great having a budget to work to, as it means I don't have to miss any payments to buy food. We are also saving too. It's so reassuring to know that when the MOT comes round we can use our own money, rather than 'robbing Peter to pay Paul' and getting behind in our debts. We have saved up for our car tax and the vet fees for my dogs. It's really empowering. I see a real future for my family – which is great.

CAP is from God. It doesn't matter about your race, religion, sexuality or circumstance – they will provide you with hope. At the end of the day, CAP have blessed my family. They helped us sort out our debt, enabling us to live. Then they led us to Christ, enabling us to live eternally. Thank you to everyone at CAP. My life is now worth living.

Brian & Pam

10. A LOVE TO SHARE

Pam's Story

I remember getting into a train. I was frightened because I didn't know where I was going. All I knew was that I was going away from my parents and I didn't know how long I would be gone. I was met at the train station by strangers who took me to a place I'd never been before. I was placed in a cold dormitory with eleven other children. I was frightened and during the night I wet my bed.

That morning I was introduced to the rest of the children in my dorm. The staff made me stand on my bed and tell everyone what had happened during the night. I felt humiliated and afraid, but this was just the start. The start of an experience that would leave me completely broken, without any sense of self worth or knowledge of what it is to know love.

My name is Pam. I was born with a lung condition which meant I was constantly in and out of hospital. It got to such a point that it was decided that I would be better off at a children's hospital in Liverpool, for kids with heart and lung disease.

One of the first memories of my life is that first night in the hospital. Little did I know what horrors I would see during my time there.

The ethos of the hospital was to teach you to fight. Everything was regimented, from showers to meals and exercise. We were taken on walks and then put to bed for two hours during the day to recover. The dormitories were simply brick walls one metre high with wire netting between the wall and the roof. This was to teach us to fight against the air and the cold. The floor was concrete and we slept on iron beds. In the winter we would have to break the ice before washing in the basins. It was a very abusive situation, there was no protection.

Despite, or perhaps because of the horrendous conditions, I formed a tight bond with the eleven children in my room. We promised each other that whatever happened, we wouldn't leave one another alone. We stuck to that promise even when death intervened.

It would happen in the night – someone would disappear and we would follow them. They would be taken to a marble room, which I later realised was a morgue, and placed on a bed. We would hide underneath the bed for the rest of the night so we would be together.

During my stay at the hospital all eleven of my companions died, including my best friend Heather. If I was capable of love at that time, it was Heather who I loved.

One snowy night, we moved all the beds into the middle of the dorm to prevent them getting covered in snow. Heather was cold, so I got into bed with her to keep her warm. When I woke up in the morning her body was as cold as ice. She had died in the night. I was only eight years old and I had woken up next to the corpse of my best friend.

I was too scared to tell my parents about the abuse as the children's hospital threatened us with punishment if we did. We only saw our parents once a month, during which they were only allowed to sit opposite us at a table. They were not allowed to touch us, in case we became attached. Crying wasn't allowed; if you cried you were shut in a room on your own.

Thankfully, my time at the hospital came to an end when I was thirteen. I'm not sure why they sent me back. Maybe they thought I wasn't going to be killed off that easily. However, even when I moved back home I lived in fear. I was too scared to say anything about what had happened because I remembered the staff at the hospital saying that if I did, I would be sent back. There was no way I wanted to go back, so I lived with this dark secret of abuse.

The scars of my years in the hospital began to take their toll. I couldn't laugh or cry and felt very angry. My mum remembers that I wouldn't even ask for a sweet.

I didn't fit in at school. At the children's hospital, they didn't see the point of educating us because we weren't expected to live. So I went to school aged thirteen unable to read or write. I wasn't allowed to do PE because of my illness.

In my family, I didn't fit in either. My brother was a baby when I left, but he was now grown up and I didn't know my parents. It must have been hard for them too I suppose, just getting this daughter back after years of separation. In talking with my dad later he confided in me that they had no choice but to let me go into the children's hospital. He had been informed by the medical authorities that if he refused and I died at home then he would be charged with neglect and consequent imprisonment.

In the January when I was thirteen, my life hit rock bottom and I literally came to a point of no return. I was brutally beaten up by a gang of teenagers on my way home from school. I suppose they picked me out because I didn't fit in and got out of doing PE. It was a horrific experience. My injuries were so severe that I had to crawl home on my hands and knees – one of the longest journeys of my life. As soon as I got home, my mother immediately rushed me into hospital.

At the hospital, they discovered that the beating had burst one of my kidneys. I remember the doctor sitting down with me and Dad and telling me the news. He gave me two options, either I left the kidney as it was and let it poison my body until I died or I could have it removed, with the risk of death if my lungs couldn't cope with the anaesthetic and stress of the operation. What a choice.

My father told me that it was my decision, saying, 'It's your life.' I decided that I had nothing to lose and chose to have the operation.

The night before the surgery, I was physically shaking with fear. I had so many questions going round my head. What was life all about? What happens when I die? Will I ever know what love is?

Then I saw one of the young men from my village come into the ward. I'd seen him around, but didn't know him very well. He came up to me and handed me a note. I was too proud to tell him I couldn't read, so I kept the note in my hand until he left. As he left he asked if he could come and visit me again. I said he could. It wasn't like I had many other friends anyway! Little did I realise that this meeting with that young man would have huge significance in more ways than one!

Plucking up my courage, I asked the nurse to read the note. I couldn't believe what she read out. The note read, 'God says you will live.'

I didn't know what to think, but I knew that I had to find out who this God was before I went into surgery. So I said to the nurse, 'How do you get to know God?' She replied, 'I don't know, but there's a Bible over there. If you point at the bits you want to hear, I will read it to you.'

I opened the Bible, not really knowing what I would find, and gingerly put my finger on a random page. The nurse read to me, 'Fear not, for I have redeemed you; (I didn't even know what that meant), I have summoned you by name; you are mine (up until that point I had never been called by my name, just my surname) when you pass through the waters I will be with you; and when you pass through the rivers, they will not sweep over you. When you walk through the fire you will not be burned.'

Every time I read those words I well up with tears; it still moves me even now.

'For I am the LORD, your God, the Holy One of Israel, your Saviour; … Since you are precious and honoured in my sight, and because I love you.' (Isaiah 43: 1-4)

As she read it I asked, 'God if you are real, will you be real to me right now? If I make it through I will give you my life hook, line and sinker.'

I know that I met God in those wards at Pontefract Hospital! I knew he was real. On the way to theatre I was speaking all this gobbledegook (which I later discovered was speaking in tongues) – I didn't know what it meant, but it felt good! God was so close to me.

I awoke from the general anaesthetic full of joy, albeit it a weary joy. I had survived! I wanted to learn more about this God whom I had met in those wards. The young man came back and taught me how to read and write. He also read scriptures to me, making me memorise sections of it at a time. It was annoying at the time, but now I can see just how beneficial it was to me!

As I grew up and became more competent in my reading and writing abilities, the young man encouraged me to apply to nursing school. He even filled in all the application forms for me. I was accepted, passed the entrance exam and started the course.

I went on to marry that young man! His name is Brian and he has been a faithful and loving husband to me ever since.

So my life started to take a new direction. I became a nurse and, against all the odds and the doctor's advice, gave birth to three sons: Paul, Adam and Daniel.

It was after the birth of my second son, Adam, that I was to have my first experience of God's miraculous healing. Even though the emotional trauma of my childhood was healing, I was still plagued by crippling illnesses caused by my lungs.

After Adam's birth, I was so ill that I couldn't even pick him up. It was awful. I had to sit down and have Adam rest on a cushion just to breast feed him. I can't tell you the agony of not being able to hold and comfort your child. I was on oxygen and the doctors gave me eighteen months to live.

However, God had other plans. We had a new pastor at our church. I'd never met him, but Brian had. He came round and said, 'God has told me things about your past and wants to heal you today!' He proceeded to tell me everything that had happened in my life, including the kid's home, which no-one knew about. He then said that God had told him not to touch me, but to tell me to start giving thanks and that God would heal me.

I didn't know what to think. Nothing like this had ever happened to me before, but out of obedience and in some confusion, I started to praise and thank God. All of a sudden, something happened which I can't explain. I could suddenly breathe deeply – something I had never done before. The first thing I did was go and pick up my baby. I started carrying Adam and walking around the house. My mother was shouting, 'put him down', but I wasn't about to lose this moment. I started singing loudly and was running up and down the stairs – it was so wonderful! I have never had trouble with my lungs since that day!

That healing did something in my spirit! I was completely different. I had never laughed until that day and I learnt how to cry. I had, as Brian said, 'turned from a mouse into a lion.' He even had to visit the pastor to ask for advice on how to cope with the new me! It must have been such a shock to him.

God never does anything without reason and he certainly used that healing to do incredible things. My neighbours were completely astounded by my miraculous recovery. They had seen how ill I was. They had seen Brian carry me up the stairs and had seen me lifeless. But suddenly I was this happy, smiling woman, singing really loudly in the driveway. Most of the neighbourhood ended up coming to church and many became Christians! It was so easy to tell them that my transformation was because of Jesus and they could see the physical evidence.

God began to use me to impact and speak truth into people's lives. I had been living in chains for so long and I didn't want others to be trapped inside prisons, not knowing Jesus.

Many people say that I am an evangelist, but I believe that God has told me I am a prophetic pastor. He tells me things about people or tells me to go somewhere and I obey.

If God tells me to go and stand by a red car, I go and do it and wait for him to tell me who to speak to. It's very simple and not complicated. I don't go into someone's home and preach the gospel. I just tell them what I believe God is saying. I don't believe I've been given a special gift, it's just a relationship with God and that means anyone can have it.

I just have to tell people about Jesus. I believe God has told me to share his love, set the captives free and see people healed – so that is what I do.'

It's Christ's love that keeps me going; I just feel so much love from Jesus. I love him so much and I am convinced of his incredible love for me. How can I not share that?

I remember the most wonderful experience I had of God's love. It was bonfire night and I had accidentally put my hand through some glass doors. It severed the fingers on my right hand, so much that they were almost sliced off. I went into emergency surgery to rebuild the severed fingers.

Even though I was under anaesthetic and in a different room, I could hear my husband Brian praying! However, the surgery was dangerous and I began to slip away. I could hear the surgeons saying, 'We're losing her, we're losing her.' It was in that instant that I saw Jesus. His eyes were like oceans of love. I just wanted to stay there forever. I just melted in his love. God's love is so wonderful.

He asked me to go back, but even though I had a wonderful husband and three beautiful children I didn't want to return. However, he then showed me a group of people. He said, when you next see me all these people standing here will be in heaven because you chose to return. So I did.

That experience confirmed my belief that I had been called to reach the lost. I then invested hours into reading and learning as much as I could. I also received full healing to my hand – there are now only scars to remind me of God's faithfulness and healing. God always leaves a sign to show that he's done something.

It was my heart to share God's love with others that made me the perfect candidate for the next season of my life, although it took me a while to realise!

I'd never heard about Christians Against Poverty, but Brian and Ian, the Pastor of the Dewsbury church, visited the charity to find out more. It never even crossed my mind to get involved.

Strangely enough, it was Brian who initially put himself forward for interview as a debt counsellor for the centre. But during the interview, Brian clearly heard God say, 'This is the job for Pam.'

I did not have a clue about computers, so I couldn't quite believe that God could be calling me to a job where IT is a key aspect of the role. God clearly has a sense of humour! However, I couldn't ignore God's calling, so went on a basic computer course.

Despite my lack of IT knowledge, CAP accepted my application and I trained as a Centre Manager for CAP in May 2004. Everyone was good at IT except for me and my computer was the only one that crashed! But one person said to me, 'Just imagine if you are in thirty homes in a year, that's thirty people who could potentially become Christians.' That was it for me – God got me on that point!

It soon became clear that this was the perfect job. It provided me with the opportunity to go into people's homes armed with God's love. I don't know of any other situation where you can walk into a home and have that kind of format to give Jesus away.

One client in particular stands out. Patricia was the third client I ever saw. When I met her, she was hiding in her bed every day and had lost the opportunity to see her grandchildren. She was recovering emotionally from the trauma of having her son try to set fire to her home with her locked inside. This son was in prison as a result. Understandably, Patricia was a completely broken woman. I sat there thinking, 'God, what an earth have you landed me in?' But I knew that he wanted to have Patricia as his child. It was just a case of asking God what he wanted me to say first.

I often get people to do things that will enable God to demonstrate himself in their life. On this occassion, I asked Patricia to name one thing that she would like God to do for her. When Patricia replied that she wanted to be able to see her grandchildren, we prayed specifically for that. Two weeks later, out of the blue, Patricia received a call from her daughter-in-law asking her to look after the children for the weekend.

She was filled with such joy and that was the event that showed Patricia who God was. It wasn't long before she became a Christian!

When you see a life so broken and held captive, and then you see that person now leading people to Christ and discipling them, it's the biggest buzz ever! Patricia is now a Support Worker voluntarily helping me and the clients. I just love it! I love asking the impossible of God and expecting him to do it! At the end of the day, how can I not give what Jesus has given to me? I have truly discovered a love worth sharing.

Pam

Pam is now one of CAP's most successful Centre Managers. Since starting in 2004, Pam has helped one-hundred-and-twenty-one clients out of debt and has led fifty clients to Christ. This includes Emily & Nigel's family, whose story you have just read in chapter nine.

Notes:

We understand that reading about Pam's experience at the children's hospital is very traumatic. After investigating the situation we have, unfortunately, discovered that this kind of treatment was current practice in the 1950s (the time Pam was in the hospital).

This form of treatment was recorded in 1919 when a medical paper recommending it was published in the British Medical Journal, 22 November 1919. In the article, Chief Medical Officer T. Hartley Martin wrote:

'*The treatment of surgical tuberculosis needs an open barren, flat shore, exposed to the full force of the winds, with a fresh and equable temperature, moderate humidity, and abundant sunshine ... In the wards the majority of the children rapidly become accustomed to the open-air life, and although, as a glance at the section plan will show, the wards cannot be heated, they [children] do not appear to feel the cold, and make light of what is often a hardship to the nursing staff ... The most marked results of the open-air life are shown during the first months of stay in hospital ... [children] soon become rosy-cheeked and contented, the appetite improves rapidly.'* (p.664, BMJ November 1919)

11. NEW FAMILY

Beverley's Story

I can remember sitting in the bank manager's office and feeling this incredible pressure. The room was hot and airless and I could hardly breathe. My heart was racing, my palms were sweaty and I couldn't think straight. My then husband was sitting next to me, urging me to sign the document that was on the desk in front of us, but everything inside me was screaming not to. Then from across the desk, the loan advisor started pressurising me too. 'Your husband needs you to sign this document,' he said, leaning closer as he spoke in an almost menacing way. 'The only way for your husband to sort out his finances is for you to sign this loan agreement.'

The tension was almost too much to bear. My heart started to beat faster. The pen was only inches from my hand, so close. I knew that all I had to do was reach out and sign the form. Just one small signature was all it would take, but then at the same time I knew it would be a massive mistake.

My hands were shaking and my husband almost stopped breathing as I reached towards the pen. He could sense that I was thinking about signing. One signature would change my future. I was desperate not to sign but I couldn't take the anger if I didn't. I reached out, taking the pen in my hand and moved towards the document. Then, all of a sudden, it was like time stood still. My husband, motionless beside me; the loan advisor, sitting behind his desk; the pen; the document; an endless list of 'what ifs' racing through my mind. We were frozen in time for an instant.

The thing is, though, I just couldn't bear the pressure any longer. I had to sign the form and it felt like the clock had stopped ticking. I made contact with the pen on the contract and then moved it in that all-too-familiar way. Suddenly, my signature was on the loan agreement. Signed. Finished. Instantly, it was like everything in the room breathed a giant sigh of relief, but inside I was in agony. What had I done? I had already racked up massive credit card bills to service my husband's debts because he couldn't afford to pay them off. But this new loan would mean an extra £408 a month coming out of my account. My husband smiled and the loan advisor looked like he'd just reeled in a prize-winning fish. I would have been more distraught, had it not been for the fact that I was numb and paralysed with fear at the same time. That was in April 2004.

In May 2006 my life was turned upside down as my husband walked out on me and our ten-year old daughter without warning. It was like my world had collapsed in front of me. The trauma and shock were almost too great to take in and my daughter was inconsolable. We were picking over the pieces of shattered dreams and I didn't know where to turn. It felt like there was no hope for us. To add insult to injury, he not only left sadness but also his debts. I felt sick with fear and anger and wanted to scream. I wanted someone to rub it all out and transport me and my daughter to a different life, away from all the financial worries and the pain. I felt like I'd been dropped into a big black hole.

In my desperation, I went to see a solicitor as I was in totally over my head. I can remember his words even to this day: 'You'll have to get rid of the house.' He knew I couldn't afford to keep the house and pay the debts at the same time, but I was so desperate to keep it. The house was a little piece of stability for me and my daughter in the midst of a storm. I earned a good salary and could always afford to pay off my debts and keep my head above water beforehand, but I couldn't keep my ex's head above water too now that I was servicing his debt as well. I was drowning, sinking further into financial ruin and it looked like there was no way out.

In spite of the solicitor's advice, I chose not to get rid of the house. I just couldn't; it was too lovely. It felt like selling it would erase the last little scrap of dignity I had left; the only remnant of a happier life and I couldn't surrender that as well. It was such a beautiful house, after all; a three-bedroom semi with a brand new kitchen and conservatory. The same solicitor said to me, 'What do you want in the divorce?' I said that I wanted my ex husband to pay his debt off, but I would absorb the debt on the house, so long as I got to keep it as my home.

So I struggled on and kept the house for a further six months before my ex dropped another bombshell. He was jealous because we were still in the house, even though he was the one who had walked away. He couldn't stand me enjoying it whilst he lived in other accommodation.

I remember the day vividly, it was during Christmas 2006 and he phoned me up and said that he wasn't going to pay his personal loan any more. He said, 'It's got your name on it, so when I stop paying it, they're going to chase after you and you'll have to give up your house.' It was devastating and I was shocked at how malicious he was being. I knew he would follow through on his threat too. Sure enough, that fateful day with my ex and the loan advisor came back to haunt me. I wished I'd never signed that loan agreement. I wished I'd stood up to the bullying and the anger and not signed. I felt like such a fool and now I was paying the price.

For a week or so after his threat, the phone was silent but then the bank started; the phone calls, the harassment, the letters through the door. It was relentless. They called me morning, noon and night. I couldn't bear the pressure of it all. The bank was chasing me for another £400 a month, which I knew I couldn't pay. It just tipped me over the edge. I had been managing to pay off the debts and keep the house, but all this was too much to take.

I had gone to church for years – it was a Church of England church in Denton, Greater Manchester, which my mum also attended. My mum was a helper at Carmel Christian Centre in Tameside and she heard that they were opening a CAP Centre. I was in despair at the time and wondered what on earth I was going to do and I can remember her words so clearly. She said, 'I've got your answer – they're opening this branch of CAP in Tameside' and she explained what the charity did to help people like me.

Sue, the Centre Manager and Denise Green, one of the CAP helpers, came to my house and sat down with me. I was so nervous before they turned up. I didn't know what to expect, but I was so desperate that I would have chosen anything to get out of the mess that I was in. I was utterly depressed and I felt like there was no hope for me or my daughter.

I will never forget the first meeting we had. I answered the door nervously when the bell rang. I welcomed Sue and Denise into the house and they sat down on the sofa. Only a few minutes into the conversation, they said the words that I had been longing to hear: 'Give us everything, we will deal with it.' It was such a relief for me to hear those words and know they would help to sort everything out. I didn't have to struggle on alone They even told me to ignore the calls from the creditors. At this time, creditors were constantly calling and calling and calling and it was wearing me down. I had to leave the answer phone on and stop paying the credit card bills so I could concentrate on the priority debts. That was so hard at first. It really tugged at my pride. I had worked for years, earned a good salary and always managed to pay things on time. To be told that I had to forego paying some of my bills temporarily was a real shock. I found it difficult, but I knew I just had to do it; it was my only way out.

It's funny how a crisis can force you to make radical, life-changing decisions even when you think you don't have the strength to. A few weeks later, I was sitting in Sue's office at the Carmel Church. I turned round to her and said in desperation, 'I've got to get out of this'. The payment plan had come back from CAP and the debt was so large, it would have taken over eighteen years to pay back. It was unacceptable to have this kind of debt hanging over my head, so I gathered up all my courage and strength and said the words I always dreamed I'd never have to, 'What about bankruptcy?' This was truly my last resort.

Once I'd uttered those frightening words Sue was so reassuring and gave me all the information I needed and I realised that it would get rid of all my debt. A member of the specialist insolvency team, John, got in contact with me shortly after. I felt real peace as he talked through everything and we decided bankruptcy was the best option for me. It was a proper solution, instead of treading financial water, but it wasn't going to be a painless process.

The next few months were really tough, in spite of all the help I had received from CAP. I was on debt management for about six months, which meant living on a tighter budget than I had before until the bankruptcy had been cleared through the courts. It was so hard. I had a ten year old daughter who wanted me to buy things for her and who was also used to doing things like going on holiday.

My relationship with my ex went from bad to worse when he announced that he was no longer going to pay maintenance for my daughter as she had refused to see him. The thing was her heart was broken when he moved out and I can understand how devastating it was for her. My daughter had been forced to move house against her will and suffer the pain of her parents' divorce. I think this was just too much for her to take. It had been so traumatic for her and I knew why she didn't want to see him. The whole situation had pushed her over the edge.

It seemed we weren't able to resolve the situation about the maintenance and my daughter not seeing my ex so he took me to court. The injustice of it made me so angry at the time; I was seething. Staff from the Child Welfare Department got involved and mediated between my ex and my daughter. The good news is that now she sees him and he has restarted paying maintenance again, but it was such a devastating experience for her. I'm so pleased it's resolved, though.

Before the bankruptcy went through, I voluntarily surrendered my keys to the estate agent in a formal arrangement. It was a bitter pill to swallow. I couldn't believe that I was finally getting rid of the house. A home that I had made, paid for and brought my daughter up in; the home that had seen many happy memories in spite of the painful ones of the previous year. Still, when a crisis hits you just have to do everything you can to get through it. Looking back, I'm almost surprised at the radical decisions I did make. I never thought that I'd have the courage to do what I did, but CAP stood by me and I knew that God was watching over me, as painful as it was.

I will never forget what happened after that. It was only about two weeks since I had given the keys back to the estate agent and not long before I was due to move out of the property. Sue had organised for her husband, son and a few other men from their church to move me in to a rented house.

On that Saturday, I woke up unaware that I was about to see a loving church in action. The men arrived at my house and I was blown away by their generosity and kindness. They did everything, including moving the furniture and I moved into a beautiful house in Denton without lifting a finger.

I was much closer to my Mum and my sisters too, which was such a relief. I'd been living further away from them in Ashton and although it was only four miles, the traffic was awful and it took ages to drive between the two. I had felt so isolated, so this move was fantastic. I moved into a lovely modern house and I will never forget the kindness of all those people from Carmel Church who helped us to move. I knew then that this house had been God-sent for me and I had to go to that church as the people had impacted my life so much.

When we moved into the new house we were still on debt management, (which was a struggle, but we were getting on with it) because the bankruptcy was about to be formalised through the courts. I was so impacted by the love and kindness of Sue, her husband and friends that I went to the church one Sunday. I walked in not knowing what to expect though and felt quite nervous.

The Missions Pastor, who used to be the full time Pastor of the church was talking and it was like he was talking directly to me. It was fantastic preaching and I know that I was meant to go that day. I have never looked back and I'm now involved with lots of activities with that church. We loved it! The look on my daughter's face when she left her Sunday school that morning will never leave me. All that pain and trauma had been washed away. She was beaming. I hadn't seen her smile like that for so long. It felt like we'd come home.

I had to go to court on 7 December to put the bankruptcy through. We had been on debt management for about nine months before this. I went to court with Mark, the Pastor of Carmel and Sue came with me too for moral support. It was a daunting process and such a horrible thing to go through, but I thought to myself,

'Just go for it, just get it done'. I wasn't worried but it was a really awful situation.

When I walked out of the courtroom, I was overjoyed. I just kept on thinking 'It's gone, it's gone.' All that debt that was hanging over my head, all that pain and struggle, all the humiliation, gone in an instant. It was like someone had removed a ten tonne weight from my head and the relief was almost overwhelming. I felt so amazing and I owed it to God and to the help of everyone from CAP.

The church has been an amazing support to both me and my daughter throughout the whole process and I've really seen how supportive and loving a church can be. The one major worry I had in moving house though, was that my daughter was coming up to the age where she was going to go to high school. There was a very good Church of England high school in Oldham that she would have almost been guaranteed a place at, had we kept attending the local Church of England church. I'm so proud of my daughter and how she has battled through what is a traumatic time in our lives. I was concerned about the school situation as she's such a bright girl and I wanted her to be happy.

One major boost was that whilst all the difficulties were happening at home, she was made head girl at her previous school. It was just the boost to her confidence that she needed and I knew it was God encouraging her through a very dark time. I thought that if we went to Carmel Church she'd struggle to get into the great school in Oldham, but I believed it was the right place for us to go. I decided to take the risk and trust God with my daughter's future. It was easier said than done, but such an important faith lesson for me.

In an act of genuine kindness, I got a really good letter from the Vicar of the Church of England church that we used to attend. It was a fantastic reference and totally supported my daughter's application to the school in Oldham, in spite of her no longer going to that church. Mark, the pastor of Carmel wrote a letter too and we filled in the application form and sent it off and waited for what seemed like months and months.

When the date drew closer and closer I was praying about it every day and we had the whole of Carmel church praying about it too. I was so nervous before we heard the decision, but God answered our prayers and she got a place at the school against all the odds. She started in September 2008. She went to the school's open evening and loved it so much. She has also decided that she wants to be a solicitor and I just know that she will make it. I'm so proud of her and I know that thanks to God working through CAP, we have a hope and a future. I can now look my daughter in the eye and say that God has been caring for us and guiding us all the way, even when we couldn't see him at work and even when things were so painful.

So what I now have is some furniture, a lease car, a rented house and you know what, I don't care. In fact I couldn't care less! I earn a good salary and with careful budgeting I can afford a few luxuries every now and then. After all that pain, it's so wonderful to see God's healing hand on our lives. He has turned everything around.

I didn't think I could do it, but Sue asked me to stand up and give my testimony a year after CAP started in Carmel Church. That morning I was helping serve breakfast before the service and I was racked with nerves. As the service began, I went to sit next to Sue and I suddenly thought to myself, 'Don't be stupid. Why are you so nervous? You're not alone, you're amongst friends.' As I spoke, people were really amazed by my testimony of how God rescued me and used people from CAP in the process.

That's the way I'd sum things up really; that I'm now amongst friends where before I was so alone. I have been given a family and a beautiful home and I've never been happier.

Pete & Maxine.

12. MARRIAGE RESTORED

Pete & Maxine's Story

I remember the day Pete proposed to me. He asked me to catch the bus to a stop in the middle of Peckham, London. Pete was waiting for me at the bus stop. He told me to close my eyes and proceeded to get down on one knee and propose to me right in front of everyone! Of course I said yes. We got married the following June after knowing each other for just eight months. It was love at first sight!

We met when we were both living in London. Pete was made president of The Rotoract Club[2] and I became his secretary. Friends kept telling me that Pete fancied me, but I was far too shy to believe them or do anything about it. Then one Saturday we went to a raft race. It was really hot and Pete's back was burning in the sun. My mate Sally told me to put some sun cream on his back. Plucking up all my courage, I went up to him and said, 'Pete, do you need some cream on your back? You're burning!' He was also shy, but let me put some sun cream on his back. Whilst I was doing it he asked me out!

I had been stood up by guys before, so kept asking him, 'Pete you will turn up won't you?' He assured me he would and we arranged to meet. The first date was great but I was so nervous! He picked me up in a cab and we did some window shopping in Peckham. Then we went to have a cup of coffee in a café. We hit it off and it was only a couple of months later when Pete proposed.

My father took a while to warm to Pete but my mother and younger brother liked him immediately. My younger brother Paul is over six foot tall and towers over Pete. They get on like a house on fire – and soon bonded over a shared love of fishing.

---

[2] A rotary club for teenagers

We spent four years in London and had three children – Judy, Lizzie and Peter (or PJ, as we call him). We stayed there until we had an incident where I was mugged and then almost mugged again on the same day. This made me feel I was no longer safe.

Also, Pete was in a wheelchair because of problems with his back and he couldn't work. Because we were living in a high-rise flat he couldn't get out very much and got very depressed. This, combined with the deterioration of the area meant that we needed to leave.

We moved back to Barnsley. Pete was still too ill to work because of his back, but he was certainly much happier than when we were in London. Life was nice in Barnsley, Lizzie was at nursery and Judy had just started school – so the kids were still very young – and we were staying in a council house. However, life was hard in some respects. We were out in the sticks and so it was hard to get into town unless we went on numerous trains and buses, but at least Pete could get out, and he even learnt to drive. Things took a turn for the worse when we were told that we had to create a drive for the car because it couldn't stay on the road. It was then that all the financial problems started. We got a loan in order to build a drive but didn't realise the impact it would have on our lives.

We then took out more loans to buy presents for the kids at Christmas and to take the family away on holiday to Scotland. It was hard to say no to the children, especially as they got older and became more and more demanding.

For a while we were doing really well and could afford all the repayments on our debts. But then we missed a payment by a few days and everything went wrong. We were struggling to pay the £30 per month we needed to pay back the debt, and each time we looked at the statement we could see that it was never going down. I went to the bank and they told me that all I was doing was paying off the interest. I asked them to stop the interest for a while in order to give us a break, which they did, but then they re-started it again. We just couldn't afford it.

What followed was a series of huge mistakes. The next December, I took out another loan to pay for Christmas, and then the TV packed in. We couldn't do without a telly so we went to one of these 'buy to view' companies. Basically, they give you a television and you pay for it over a period of several years.

Things got worse when three months later, the tumble dryer broke down. All my bairns (children) were at school, and I needed a dryer to get their uniforms ready each day. So we went back to the same company for a new one.

Another two months passed, and then the washing machine went. We got someone to look at it and paid £80 to get the ball bearings sorted, only for it to pack up a few months later. It was going to cost another £80 and so I decided to get a new washing machine from our 'buy to view' company.

As we were doing so well with our payments, the 'buy to view' company offered us another, bigger and better TV. We thought we might as well go for it, as we had nearly finished paying for the first TV. However, unbeknown to us, every time you get any new item, the price left on your other equipment is reduced, but the payment term is lengthened. This means that if you default on any payments, they can take the lot back. It was 2001 that we got our first television and we still haven't paid it off. Every month I have to pay £100 just to keep everything working.

The burden of all this, combined with the various loans just got too much. At the start I'd manage to hold off the creditors from court action, but then the letters and phone calls started. We had nearly £6,000 worth of debt.

By this time we had moved to Wingate, near Durham – a place we'd fallen in love with after visiting my sister-in-law. It's close to the beaches and just an amazing place to live. Neither of us were working as Pete was unable to work and I was his carer and housewife.

The sheer burden of the debt almost broke us as a family. We didn't know how to talk to one another, so we just shouted and took all our frustration out on each other. The fighting and arguing over bills was constant. Not just between me and Pete, but also the kids. Our house was just a place of anger and fighting. The fights were so bad that we had punch marks in the doors, and holes from where we'd kicked them in. I would just scream at Pete and him at me – it was terrible and a long way from the happy days of our wedding.

We'd wake up, but wouldn't want to get out of bed. Then the post would arrive. I couldn't bear the sight of all the bills. But what I couldn't stand even more was Pete continually going on about them. I just wanted to hit him. Then the phone calls would start. Some days we hid the phones so we couldn't hear them. I just wanted it all to go away.

Both me and Pete were falling into deep depression. We were both on anti-depressants and both had suicidal thoughts. At one point it was a case of 'who will do it first'? We just hated life and everything to do with it.

At one point we decided to sit the children down and tell them everything. We told them that we were in so much trouble and had racked up at least £10k worth of debt. I dread to think what was going through their heads as they heard this while watching their parents quite literally falling apart. I knew the kids found it hard not to have nice things or go out with their friends, and that made it so difficult.

The events that followed that day only served to make life even worse. My mother died and then, two days after the funeral, my eldest daughter Judy moved out to live with my sister-in-law because she couldn't stand to live with us any more. I felt so betrayed that I had a nervous breakdown and actually hit my sister-in-law. I was so full of anger that it just spilled out. I felt like I couldn't trust anyone. All I could see was darkness. It was like being in a black hole with no way of getting out. I thought nothing could ever change.

In the midst of all this, Pete and I decided that we no longer wanted to be together. The sceptics were going to be proved right. I wanted to be as far away from him as possible. I just felt that our marriage wouldn't survive and so I started looking at houses down in Plymouth where I'm originally from. Pete started looking at houses in Barnsley. We even started filling in the forms to apply for new homes.

Just when we were at our lowest point and I'd started therapy, we learnt about CAP from our sister-in-law. She had been through bankruptcy and CAP had really helped her.

It was with some trepidation that I picked up the phone. I was so low that I couldn't believe anything good could possibly happen. I felt very 'iffy' about the whole thing, but thought I'd give it a go. It was the stigma of being in debt that made me cautious. I felt like we would be judged for failing to handle our finances well enough.

When Janet (Durham Centre Manager) and CAP got involved things began to change and we started to feel lighter. She put us at ease straight away and didn't make us feel judged either. CAP sorted out all the repayments for us and set up an account that we just have to pay a set amount into. As a result all our bills and debts got sorted. When

Janet told us about all the other people she and CAP were helping we felt much better. We thought that if CAP were able to help others in our situation, including Pete's sister and dad, then maybe they can help us too. So, I started to trust CAP and Janet.

Even though creditors would ring and lie to us saying that CAP weren't doing things, I just knew that CAP could be trusted. I told these creditors to deal with CAP not us and would just send all the post directly to CAP. With CAP taking the burden, it allowed me and Pete to sort out our marriage. Because we didn't have the stress of the threatening letters, we didn't argue about our debt and were able to start talking to each other rather than shouting. We were starting to act like a real couple again.

In June 2007, we had the most wonderful experience. CAP said they would take us away on holiday! We hadn't been on holiday as a family for seven years! CAP took us and some other clients to a place called Hayes, in the beautiful Derbyshire countryside. Whilst we were on the break all our worries and stress just vanished. Even the kids noticed it. We had more fun in those four days with no TV, videos or computer games, than we'd ever had on other holidays! It was amazing – we didn't have a single argument. They even took us to Alton Towers and even though it poured down with rain we had an incredible time. The kids just loved it. They went on all the rides and didn't want to go home!

The atmosphere on the holiday was amazing. It was calm and relaxed. Plus, no-one judged us because we were all in the same boat. There was just something so different about the staff too – they were great! Mixing with CAP people changed my vision about the Church and I thought that there might just be something good in it.

We even had our own mini miracle during the break. We didn't have much spending money, just a tenner for the trip. However, when we were at Alton Towers, Pete's canoe capsized and he lost the tenner from his pocket. We were so anxious because it was all we had. I went off to the laundrette to try and see if the note had got stuck inside the trouser pocket and Pete went to a meeting.

Matt Barlow was speaking and talked about a £20 note. He scrunched it up, trampled on it with his shoes and even wiped it under his arm pit! He said that you could use this £20 note to do anything: pay a prostitute, buy drugs etc. At the end of the talk Matt offered the £20 to anyone who wanted it. He said that it didn't matter what the £20 note had done – it was still worth £20. Despite the fact it was dirty and had been used for bad purposes, it still could be used for good. Matt said that was how God sees us. It didn't matter what we had done or how dirty we felt, God still valued and loved us the same. No-one took it, so he offered it to Pete, who said, 'Yeah I'll have that!' At the end of the meeting, Pete went to give it back to Matt, but he told him he could keep it! Matt had no idea that we'd lost £10 that day. So we lost £10, but gained £20!

Pete had been born into a Catholic family and his mum's sister was a nun. He used to go to church because his mates did, but stopped as soon as he was old enough. He was just disillusioned with it all.

However, after the break we decided there was definitely something there and thought we'd give Emmanuel Church a try. This is the church Janet goes to. Going to church was a bit strange at first, but we got used to it and began to feel part of the place. It just kept getting better and each time I went I saw a bit more light in my life. I started to feel more positive and the atmosphere at home even began to change.

We stopped swearing at each other and the arguments subsided. Now, if I don't go to church I feel like something is missing.

We soon decided to become Christians after the break. It took us time and it was a gradual decision. We just began to feel more comfortable and realised that this is what we really wanted. To be honest it was the break away that clinched the deal for us, even though it took some time for us to make the final decision.

Once we became Christians, it felt like a huge weight had been lifted from our shoulders. Emotionally, Pete used to lock everything away and let it build up until he exploded. But now when he has problems, he talks to God and to people. Pete keeps a Bible in the car and reads it when I do the shopping. Lots of things make sense to him now and it's great to see him smiling so much.

Because of CAP and the church, our lives are so different now. I am so much more relaxed. I see light now, not darkness! We are so happy. Our marriage has also been made stronger through going to church. When Pete and I go to church we hold hands – we never used to do that. We talk to each other like a couple should and just love each other so much. We celebrated our twentieth wedding anniversary in June! Who would have thought it after all we've been through. We only went to McDonald's, but I couldn't stop smiling! I was just so happy.

The kids are happier too and don't get on our nerves like they used to. They are much less stressed and wound up. PJ used to be such a terror and so unpleasant to have around, but he is turning into a lovely lad. Lizzie is great too, she can see such a difference in us. She can see that we no longer want to, in her words, 'kill each other' and are actually talking to one another. We can now leave PJ and Lizzie alone in the house together, without fear of what might happen.

We've even come back to see that they've cleaned the house – a definite miracle! I adore my kids and I am so happy to see them doing well and enjoying life.

Pete and PJ have started cycling with each other in the evenings. They are even doing little jobs together like rebuilding the fence, turfing the lawn or fixing the car. PJ loves mechanics and is great with cars.

We've even made new wonderful friends. We've been out bowling as a family with people from church and have been to a BBQ at our friend Brian's house. Janet even gave us her old car when she was got a new one! Life is just so great.

We have a new philosophy in life if things don't go right. 'God gives you what you need, not what you want.' We are applying that to all areas of our life. We are budgeting and saving now. As a family we are looking to the future and moving on from the past. Pete is training in computers to try and get back into work again, and has already passed two exams! We have also replaced the doors broken by our fights as a sign of the future and are even saving up for a holiday in Spain to see my youngest brother Paul. He promised to take Pete fishing years ago, but we've never been able to afford the visit!

Thinking back over my life, I just can't believe how much it has changed since that wonderful day when Pete proposed. We've been through such turmoil, but someone was looking out for us. CAP was a complete lifesaver and in just under three years we will be debt-free! The honest truth is that if we hadn't had CAP, our family would have been destroyed. I can't thank CAP and God enough for saving my life and that of my family.

John & Lizzie with (from left) Jasmine, Abigail, Simon, Lydia, Tom & Jessica.

EPILOGUE

By John Kirkby

So there you are, twelve amazing stories. To be honest if these were the only lives changed over the last few years, I think all the challenges and struggles we faced would still have been worth it. As I read about their lives, the devastation and the heartbreak they faced and then read how God has used us to change those situations so miraculously, I am left with an incredible sense of joy and excitement about what God has done, is doing and will do through CAP as we press forward.

In many ways my own journey of hope is reflected in so many of the stories you've read. My story began in 1992 when I lost everything and faced life alone, destitute, in debt, lonely and broken. From that depth of despair, God reached into one lonely man's life with overwhelming love and compassion. I gave my life to God in 1994 and from that time, God rebuilt me from the inside out. I realised that God had a purpose for my life and a future for me and my two beautiful daughters, Jasmine and Jessica.

I could never have known all those years ago that God would use that darkness to bring light to others. By enabling me to climb out of the hole into which I'd fallen, God helped me do for myself what CAP was about to do for thousands of other people.* At the beginning of 1996, I began to realise that although God had given me a new life and hope, there was more that he wanted to do with me. He wanted me to use my experience to help the poor. So in June 1996, with my new wife Lizzie, I started Christians Against Poverty just after returning from our honeymoon.

---

*You can read more of John's story in his book 'Nevertheless'. Get your free copy by registering on line at www.capuk.org.

I clearly remember my second client. I went to see Debbie Thompson in October 1996. I remember sitting in her lounge hearing of a family whose life was totally devastated and her struggle to feed her two sons Lloyd and Adam, aged nine and seven respectively. You can imagine the joy it is for me to read Lloyd's story some twelve years later in this book. It inspires me to think of the long-term impact this work will have and is having, as the hope of thousands of families is played out throughout generations.

As a family our journey of hope continues to unfold. Lizzie and I have three beautiful children; Abigail, Thomas and Lydia. An incredible future is unfolding for Jasmine and Jessica. Jasmine was seven when I was at our lowest point, but she has come through to finish university with a First Class degree and now works here at CAP. She is married to a great Christian guy, and has got an incredible future ahead of her in God. Jessica was so young and so innocent in the midst of my life collapsing, but she too has come through so strong and has just started at university on a midwifery course – a miracle and her heart's desire. As always, Lizzie, my wonderful wife, is right by my side. She is my rock and I so appreciate all that she is and does. I'm sure you all realise now that one family's journey of hope is not just for those people, but it's for the generations that follow. Lizzie and I look forward to seeing joy continue to unfold in our family's future.

So how is CAP able to bring about such transformation in thousands of lives? I've known the answer to this ever since I started in my bedroom with a tenner. I knew hope was in God, but I also knew that to release hope into the lives of others, I needed people. I needed people to join and support what we were doing, I needed people to pray and to give, and people to sacrificially lay down their lives to change this nation one life at a time. The unsung heroes of this amazing work and thousands of lives transformed are our staff, volunteers, supporters and churches that partner with us throughout the UK. Without their dedication, sacrifice, hard work and determination to reach the poor with the gospel of hope, all our hopes and dreams would have come to nothing and this book could never have been written.

Andy Jackson's story epitomises what it is that God is looking for in all our lives – a heart for others. A heart that puts other people's needs before their own, a heart that can do all things through God who strengthens them, a heart to do all they can for the lost and broken. It's through literally thousands of people like Andy that our ministry has grown to what it is today. As you reflect on the stories you've read, my heart is that you will be inspired to do what you can do. Can you pray for us? Can you support us financially with just a few pounds a month and join our Life Changer programme? Can you get involved either directly with your local church or inspire your church to get involved in the work of CAP? You need to know that we need you, the church needs you, the poor and needy in communities need you, and God needs you to fulfil his heart of justice and mercy for the poor of this nation. Do it today, don't delay! Fill in a Life Changer form from the back of this book, get on the website, join the prayer team or contact your pastor. Do it soon, don't let anything get in the way of you joining and supporting us to see thousands more 'journeys of hope' unfold.

Thank you

John Kirkby, Founder & International Director

BECOME A LIFE Changer

AND HELP MORE JOURNEYS OF HOPE UNFOLD...

YOUR DETAILS

Title .... First Name .... Surname ....

Address ....

.... Postcode ....

Phone number .... am /pm Email ....

Where did you get this form? ....

YOUR GIFT

I/We would like to make a monthly gift of £3   £5   £10   £20   £50   or £.......

on the   **1st   8th   15th   28th**   **(please select)** of each month until further notice.

The first payment will be made in .... (please state month)

GIFT AID DECLARATION

I am a UK taxpayer and I would like Christians Against Poverty to reclaim tax on all my donations as from the 1st April 2007.*

Signature: ....   Signature: ....

Date: _ _ / _ _ / _ _

*You must pay income tax and/or capital gains tax at least equal to the amount we claim on your donation in the tax year (currently 28p for every £1 that you give). Please notify Christians Against Poverty if you change your name and/or address. Reg. Charity Nº 1097217.

CHRISTIANS AGAINST POVERTY UK

Instruction to your Bank/Building Society to pay by Direct Debit

DIRECT Debit

Originators Identification Nº: 8 3 7 3 8 5

Please return to: Supporter Relations Team, CAP, Jubilee Mill, North Street, Bradford, BD1 4EW (registered office)

Name and full postal address of your Bank/Building Society

To: The Manager:
Bank/Building Society: ....

Address: ....

Postcode: ....

Instruction to your Bank/Building Society

Please pay Christians Against Poverty Direct Debits from the account detailed in this instruction, subject to the safeguards assured by the Direct Debit Guarantee. I understand that this instruction may remain with Christians Against Poverty and if so details will be passed electronically to my bank/building society.

Name(s) of account holder(s) ....

Branch Sort Code ☐☐☐☐☐☐   Bank/building society account number ☐☐☐☐☐☐☐☐   Ref: (office use only) ☐☐☐☐☐☐☐☐

Signature: ....   Date: _ _ / _ _ / _ _

Banks and Building Societies may not accept Direct Debit instructions for some types of account

Registered charity No. 1097217 Charity Registered in Scotland No. SC038776 Company Limited by Guarantee, Registered in England and Wales No. 4655175

The Direct Debit Guarantee: The Direct Debit Guarantee should be detached and retained by the payer.

This guarantee is offered by all Banks and Building Societies that take part in the Direct Debit scheme. The efficiency and security of the scheme is monitored and protected by your own Bank or Building Society. If the amounts to be paid or the payment dates change, Christians Against Poverty will notify you 10 working days in advance of your account being debited or as otherwise agreed. If an error is made by Christians Against Poverty or your Bank or Building Society, you are guaranteed a full and immediate refund from your branch of the amount paid. You can cancel a Direct Debit at any time by writing to your Bank or Building Society. Please also send a copy of your letter to us.

BECOME A

LIFE Changer

 CHRISTIANS AGAINST POVERTY [UK]

AND HELP MORE JOURNEYS OF HOPE UNFOLD...

YOUR DETAILS

Title .... First Name .... Surname ....

Address ....

.... Postcode ....

Phone number .... am /pm Email ....

Where did you get this form? ....

YOUR GIFT

I/We would like to make a monthly gift of £3 £5 £10 £20 £50 or £.......

on the **1st 8th 15th 28th (please select)** of each month until further notice.

The first payment will be made in .... (please state month)

GIFT AID DECLARATION

I am a UK taxpayer and I would like Christians Against Poverty to reclaim tax on all my donations as from the 1st April 2007.*

Signature: .... Signature: ....

Date: _ _ / _ _ / _ _

*You must pay income tax and/or capital gains tax at least equal to the amount we claim on your donation in the tax year (currently 28p for every £1 that you give). Please notify Christians Against Poverty if you change your name and/or address. Reg. Charity N° 1097217.

CHRISTIANS AGAINST POVERTY [UK]

Instruction to your Bank/Building Society to pay by Direct Debit

DIRECT Debit

Originators Identification N°: 8 3 7 3 8 5

Please return to: Supporter Relations Team, CAP, Jubilee Mill, North Street, Bradford, BD1 4EW (registered office)

Name and full postal address of your Bank/Building Society

To: The Manager:
Bank/Building Society: .... Address: ....

.... Postcode: ....

Instruction to your Bank/Building Society

Please pay Christians Against Poverty Direct Debits from the account detailed in this instruction, subject to the safeguards assured by the Direct Debit Guarantee. I understand that this instruction may remain with Christians Against Poverty and if so details will be passed electronically to my bank/building society.

Name(s) of account holder(s) ....

Branch Sort Code	Bank/building society account number	Ref: (office use only)
☐☐☐☐☐☐	☐☐☐☐☐☐☐☐	☐☐☐☐☐☐☐

Signature: .... Date: _ _ / _ _ / _ _

Banks and Building Societies may not accept Direct Debit instructions for some types of account

Registered charity No. 1097217 Charity Registered in Scotland No. SC038776 Company Limited by Guarantee, Registered in England and Wales No. 4655175

- -

The Direct Debit Guarantee: The Direct Debit Guarantee should be detached and retained by the payer. **DIRECT Debit**

This guarantee is offered by all Banks and Building Societies that take part in the Direct Debit scheme. The efficiency and security of the scheme is monitored and protected by your own Bank or Building Society. If the amounts to be paid or the payment dates change, Christians Against Poverty will notify you 10 working days in advance of your account being debited or as otherwise agreed. If an error is made by Christians Against Poverty or your Bank or Building Society, you are guaranteed a full and immediate refund from your branch of the amount paid. You can cancel a Direct Debit at any time by writing to your Bank or Building Society. Please also send a copy of your letter to us.

BECOME A

LIFE
Changer

AND HELP MORE JOURNEYS OF HOPE UNFOLD...

CHRISTIANS
AGAINST POVERTY UK

YOUR DETAILS

Title .... First Name .... Surname ....

Address ....

.... Postcode ....

Phone number .... am /pm Email ....

Where did you get this form? ....

YOUR GIFT

I/We would like to make a monthly gift of £3 £5 £10 £20 £50 or £.......

on the **1st 8th 15th 28th** **(please select)** of each month until further notice.

The first payment will be made in .... (please state month)

GIFT AID DECLARATION

I am a UK taxpayer and I would like Christians Against Poverty to reclaim tax on all my donations as from the 1st April 2007.*

Signature: .... Signature: ....

Date: _ _ / _ _ / _ _

*You must pay income tax and/or capital gains tax at least equal to the amount we claim on your donation in the tax year (currently 28p for every £1 that you give). Please notify Christians Against Poverty if you change your name and/or address. Reg. Charity N° 1097217.

CHRISTIANS
AGAINST POVERTY UK

**Instruction to your Bank/Building Society
to pay by Direct Debit**

DIRECT Debit

Originators Identification N°: 8 3 7 3 8 5

Please return to: Supporter Relations Team, CAP, Jubilee Mill, North Street, Bradford, BD1 4EW (registered office)

Name and full postal address of your Bank/Building Society

To: The Manager:
Bank/Building Society: ....

Address:

....

Postcode:

Instruction to your Bank/Building Society

Please pay Christians Against Poverty Direct Debits from the account detailed in this instruction, subject to the safeguards assured by the Direct Debit Guarantee. I understand that this instruction may remain with Christians Against Poverty and if so details will be passed electronically to my bank/building society.

Name(s) of account holder(s) ....

Branch Sort Code ☐☐ ☐☐ ☐☐   Bank/building society account number ☐☐☐☐☐☐☐☐   Ref: (office use only) ☐☐☐☐☐☐☐☐

Signature: ....   Date: _ _ / _ _ / _ _

Banks and Building Societies may not accept Direct Debit instructions for some types of account

Registered charity No. 1097217 Charity Registered in Scotland No. SC038776 Company Limited by Guarantee, Registered in England and Wales No. 4655175

The Direct Debit Guarantee: The Direct Debit Guarantee should be detached and retained by the payer.

DIRECT Debit

This guarantee is offered by all Banks and Building Societies that take part in the Direct Debit scheme. The efficiency and security of the scheme is monitored and protected by your own Bank or Building Society. If the amounts to be paid or the payment dates change, Christians Against Poverty will notify you 10 working days in advance of your account being debited or as otherwise agreed. If an error is made by Christians Against Poverty or your Bank or Building Society, you are guaranteed a full and immediate refund from your branch of the amount paid. You can cancel a Direct Debit at any time by writing to your Bank or Building Society. Please also send a copy of your letter to us.

BECOME A **LIFE Changer**

CHRISTIANS
AGAINST POVERTY UK

AND HELP MORE JOURNEYS OF HOPE UNFOLD...

YOUR DETAILS

Title .... First Name .... Surname ....

Address ....

.... Postcode ....

Phone number .... am /pm Email ....

Where did you get this form? ....

YOUR GIFT

I/We would like to make a monthly gift of £3   £5   £10   £20   £50   or £.......

on the **1st   8th   15th   28th   (please select)** of each month until further notice.

The first payment will be made in .... (please state month)

GIFT AID DECLARATION

I am a UK taxpayer and I would like Christians Against Poverty to reclaim tax on all my donations as from the 1st April 2007.*

Signature: ....   Signature: ....

Date: _ _ / _ _ / _ _

*You must pay income tax and/or capital gains tax at least equal to the amount we claim on your donation in the tax year (currently 28p for every £1 that you give). Please notify Christians Against Poverty if you change your name and/or address. Reg. Charity N° 1097217.

CHRISTIANS
AGAINST POVERTY UK

**Instruction to your Bank/Building Society
to pay by Direct Debit**

DIRECT Debit

Originators Identification N°: 8 3 7 3 8 5

Please return to: Supporter Relations Team, CAP, Jubilee Mill, North Street, Bradford, BD1 4EW (registered office)

Name and full postal address of your Bank/Building Society

To: The Manager: Address:
Bank/Building Society:
....
                                              Postcode:
....

Instruction to your Bank/Building Society

Please pay Christians Against Poverty Direct Debits from the account detailed in this instruction, subject to the safeguards assured by the Direct Debit Guarantee. I understand that this instruction may remain with Christians Against Poverty and if so details will be passed electronically to my bank/building society.

Name(s) of account holder(s) ....

Branch Sort Code   Bank/building society account number   Ref: (office use only)
☐☐ ☐☐ ☐☐   ☐☐☐☐☐☐☐☐   ☐☐☐☐☐☐☐☐☐

Signature: ....   Date: _ _ / _ _ / _ _

Banks and Building Societies may not accept Direct Debit instructions for some types of account

Registered charity No. 1097217 Charity Registered in Scotland No. SC038776 Company Limited by Guarantee, Registered in England and Wales No. 4655175

- -

The Direct Debit Guarantee: The Direct Debit Guarantee should be detached and retained by the payer.

DIRECT Debit

This guarantee is offered by all Banks and Building Societies that take part in the Direct Debit scheme. The efficiency and security of the scheme is monitored and protected by your own Bank or Building Society. If the amounts to be paid or the payment dates change, Christians Against Poverty will notify you 10 working days in advance of your account being debited or as otherwise agreed. If an error is made by Christians Against Poverty or your Bank or Building Society, you are guaranteed a full and immediate refund from your branch of the amount paid. You can cancel a Direct Debit at any time by writing to your Bank or Building Society. Please also send a copy of your letter to us.

HOW CAN I BECOME A CHRISTIAN?

We hope that you've been encouraged and uplifted by reading these twelve amazing real-life accounts. At Christians Against Poverty, we put one hundred per cent effort into providing the best possible debt counselling for all our clients. Every week we hear story after story of how they have become debt free with our help and support, becoming people who can now look forward to a life of peace and freedom from financial worry.

However, we also believe in a greater peace and freedom that is available to all of us. It doesn't just last for a lifetime, but forever. As a Christian charity, we believe that we can have eternal life through Jesus, God's son. God is perfect, he loves us very much and wants to have a close relationship with us. The problem is we've all done wrong things called sin, which have separated us from God. Jesus, God's only son, was sent to earth as the answer to our sin.

When Jesus died on the cross, he took the punishment for all the wrong we have done and will ever do. Because Jesus assumed responsibility for our wrong thoughts, words and actions, our relationship with God can be restored. All we have to do is admit the wrong we've done and ask for God's forgiveness because of what Jesus achieved on the cross.

Many of the clients in this book have not only seen their finances transformed, but also their eternal destiny. We believe in life after death and that all those who believe in Jesus can look forward to eternity with him, where everything will be perfect in spite of the pain and difficulty we have experienced in this life. Becoming a Christian is not about studying the right books, being clever or looking for a way out. It's about relationship with a God who loves us so much, he gave his only son so that we could be forgiven and enjoy being with him for eternity.

If you would like to become a Christian, it's very simple. Believe that Jesus died in your place, say sorry for the things you've done wrong (the Bible calls this repentance) and ask for his forgiveness and power to live a brand new life. You may also want to pray this prayer out loud to guide you as you do this:

Lord Jesus Christ
I am sorry for the things I have done wrong in my life
(take a few minutes to ask his forgiveness for anything particular
that is on your conscience). Please forgive me.
I now turn from everything which I know is wrong.
Thank you that you died on the cross for me so that I could be
forgiven and set free. Thank you that you offer me forgiveness and
the gift of your Spirit. I now receive that gift. Please come into my life
by your Holy Spirit to be with me forever.
Thank you Lord Jesus. Amen*

* © Alpha International 2008